D1377102

The World's Best

FISHING STORIES

The World's Best

FISHING STORIES

edited by
COLIN KEARNS

FIELD&STREAM

weldon**owen**

weldon**owen**

© 2014 Weldon Owen Inc.

1045 Sansome Street
San Francisco, CA 94111
weldonowen.com

Library of Congress Control Number
on file with the publisher.

ISBN 13: 978-1-61628-867-9
ISBN 10: 1-61628-867-1
10 9 8 7 6 5 4 3 2 1
2015 2016 2017 2018
Printed in China by 1010 Printing International

Cover and interior design by William Mack
Illustrations by SlipFloat (cover), Mike Sudal (page 12-13),
Jack Unruh (29, 56, 111, 144, 153), Vector Pro (pages 5, 9, 15, 79, 161) and Andrew
Wright (pages 40, 94, 126, 164, 177)

CONTENTS

QUEST

COMPANY

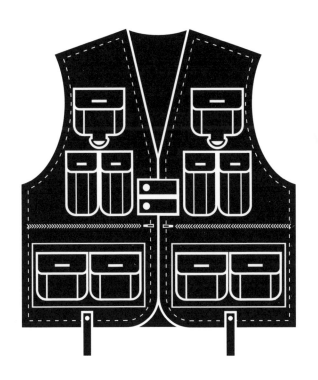

INTRODUCTION

Fishermen are born storytellers. We spend hours at tackle shops, with no intention of buying a thing, just to hear and share stories. After we release a fish, we begin collecting and constructing the details of the catch, polishing the tale for its debut. On days when we get skunked, we at least come home with a story—even if it's one we keep forever to ourselves. On days when we are not fishing, we craft stories that grant us excuses to hit the water—even if it's only for a half-hour. We allow ourselves "one last cast..." not as a curfew warning, but because we're well aware of what a great story we'd land if we hooked a fish on the last cast.

It's no wonder, really, how "fish story" earned a place in the dictionary.

This book, though, is a collection of fishing stories; not fish stories. Yes, there's a difference. I'll do my best to explain.

Don't get me wrong: There's a time and place for a good fish story. They're fun to share at camp or over beers at the bar—to hear genuine laughter from your friends at the punch lines you've perfected over the years, to watch their eyes roll as the fish inevitably, magically, gets bigger and takes longer to net with each retelling. We've all told a fish story, because we all have a fish story. And therein lies the biggest knock against them: If you've heard one fish story, you've heard them all.

A fishing story, though, has a life all its own. Whether or not the line in the water comes tight or breaks doesn't matter in a fishing story, because a fishing story, in the end, is not about catching fish. What matters in a fishing story is the quest—one on which you meet rich characters, explore new wild places, and encounter challenges you never expected.

For 120 years, *Field & Stream* has sought to find only the top-tier fishing stories, and this anthology comprises the very best of those published from the last decade. The pieces here—written by Jim Harrison, Bill Heavey, John Merwin, Thomas McGuane, Phillip Caputo, and other *F&S* favorites—tell tales of the fish that drive us to obsession, of the adventures we take to chase those obsessions, and of the families and friends who share our obsessions. It would be a crime to diminish this book as a collection of "fish stories," but it also seems dishonest not to at least acknowledge the one trait that these best fishing stories share in common with the best fish stories:

They are incredible.

Colin Kearns
Executive Editor, *Field & Stream*

OBSESSION

CHASING THE BEAST

MONTE BURKE

You probably heard the story of the 25-pound largemouth—the fish that rocked the bass scene, showed up on SportsCenter, and looked like a sure thing to shatter the 74-year-old world record. But what you might not have heard is the story of three men who have dedicated their lives to finding this fish, spending over 200 days a year on one small lake. And ultimately why, when they finally found what they were looking for, they turned their back on the dream.

The story begins in the first week of March on Dixon Lake in Escondido, California, a reservoir full of clear Colorado River water, there to slake the thirst of San Diego's suburbs. Dixon seems incapable of doing anything more significant than that. All told, it's only 70 featureless acres. In a rented Velco aluminum boat powered by a trolling motor, you can go from one end to the other in under 10 minutes. But size isn't everything.

Or is it?

An old man, a lake regular whom everyone calls "Six Pack," mans his usual post on what's known as the handicap dock at Dixon. It's morning, and the fog has just begun to burn off the hills. The old man holds a light spinning rod rigged with 2-pound-test. On the point of a small hook he's stuck a BB-size ball of Power Bait. He's fishing for trout, and Dixon is a good place to do that. Some 30,000 pounds of rainbow trout are planted in the tiny lake each year, courtesy of the California Department of Fish and Game. Fishermen aren't the only beneficiaries. "Nobody feeds their bass as well as we do," says lake ranger Jim Dayberry.

The old man already has a few good ones on his stringer when his bobber starts to dance again. He lifts his rod and sets the hook, gently, because of the light line. He reels, feeling a rhythmic pulse. He lets his mind wander a bit, thinking ahead to the trout fillets he'll eat that night.

But just as he has it nearly in, the hooked trout goes berserk, zigging and zagging in wild figure eights. There's an explosion of water, and the light tug of the trout is suddenly gone, replaced by a brutish grab that seems to want to pull him, the dock, the sky in with it. He spots his trout in the maw of something impossibly large. In a second, the pull is gone. The old man is left with his frayed line coiled like a pig's tail, his rod lifeless, his mouth agape. Later that morning, Six Pack stutters as he tries to recount the tale to a dock attendant. No one believes him. And no one realizes it at the time, but the old man had just hooked the biggest bass in the world.

Over a week later, on March 19, a cool Sunday morning, Jed Dickerson, 33, and Kyle Malmstrom, 34, are in line at the concession stand at Dixon Lake, waiting to get their permits. Dickerson is at the very front, Malmstrom just a step behind. They each fork over $30, then hustle down to the dock to the rented boats, the only type allowed. They race to attach their trolling motors. Malmstrom is the first one off. He heads north. Dickerson glances over at the handicap dock. It's one of his go-to spots, but three trout anglers are fishing from the shore nearby. He decides not to bother them and heads east.

For the past five years, Dickerson, along with his two best friends, Mac Weakley, 33, and Mike "Buddha" Winn, 32, have been chasing the next world-record largemouth bass. Their dedication to this pursuit has hurtled from pastime into obsession. Working flexible nighttime hours in the casino industry has allowed them to fish nearly 800 days among the three of them in those five years, on Dixon and a handful of other San Diego reservoirs that are the epicenter of the hunt for the world-record bass. Their persistence has reaped rewards. In 2003, Weakley caught a 19-pound 8-ounce bass from Dixon, good enough for 12th place on the list of the top 25 biggest largemouths ever recorded. Later that same year, Dickerson landed the fourth-largest bass of all time, a 21-pound 11-ounce monster, also from Dixon. The trio is well known for their dedication and skill. Dickerson has always been the most fervent of the three, the one for whom the quest has taken on its own life. He's out here early on this Sunday morning as Weakley and Winn sleep in.

Malmstrom is also a record hunter, though his obsession is limited by his nine-to-five job as an estate-planning consultant. But he has caught some notable bass, including one close to 15 pounds. He speaks in a laid-back drawl and spends most of his free time at Dixon. "You always get that magical feeling going up there that any day could be the day," he says.

On this morning, he drives his boat backward, led by his trolling motor. It's the preferred style of Dixon's big-bass hunters, providing precise control and clear sight lines into the water. He works the shoreline, peering into the depths, searching for the cleared-off rings that indicate a bass bed.

He comes around to the handicap dock. The spot is now empty. Just as Malmstrom nears the dock, he sees a massive shadow shoot from the shallows under his boat and into the deep water. "My first thought was 'Holy crap, that's an 18-plus,'" he says. He anchors on the shore, waits for 15 minutes, then idles over to see if she's returned. He spots her, maybe 10 feet away, slowly inching back to the nest. "Then I decide to wait her out," Malmstrom says. For two hours he sits, far enough away not to spook her again but close enough to guard his spot from other anglers, especially Dickerson.

At 9 a.m., he can't wait any longer and motors over. He sees the bass hovering above her nest and feels a shot of adrenaline. Tying the front of his boat to the dock, he drops an anchor off the back. The day has cleared and there's no wind on the water: perfect sight-fishing conditions. Malmstrom casts for the fish, throwing jigs and swimbaits, teasing the lures across the nest, trying to agitate her into striking.

After two hours of fruitless casting, he's tense and excited and can no longer keep his find to himself. He does something he will later regret:

He calls Dickerson on his cell phone. The two men, though they compete for the same fish, have a cordial relationship. "I'm on a big one," he boasts. Dickerson, who's on the other side of the lake, immediately relays that information to Weakley and Winn, who are now awake.

Weakley and Winn show up at the handicap dock at 1 p.m. Dickerson joins them, and they watch Malmstrom throw casts over the enormous bass. A local teenager, Dan Barnett, his interest piqued by the commotion, joins the party of onlookers. Malmstrom knows this is a special bass and decides that he will fish for her all day if he has to. But he has a problem—he needs to call his wife to tell her he won't be home anytime soon, and his cell phone has just died. He asks Weakley if he can borrow his. They work out a trade: Weakley will let him use his phone if Malmstrom will show him the fish. Malmstrom makes his call, then Weakley jumps in the boat and gets his first good look at the bass. "My God," he says, "that's Jed's fish," recognizing it as the 21-pound 11-ounce bass that Dickerson had caught three years earlier.

Back on the dock, Weakley, lusting after what he knows is at least a 20-pounder, begins pestering Malmstrom. "Come on, give me a shot. I guarantee you I can catch it." Malmstrom refuses. Weakley offers him $1,000 for 30 minutes on the fish, showing a roll of $100 bills to Barnett on the dock. Malmstrom refuses again. "I wouldn't have been able to live with myself," he says, "if Mac caught that fish."

He stays until dark but leaves the lake empty-handed. The big bass might have hit his jig once, he thinks, but he isn't sure. He's bone-tired. He contemplates calling in sick the next day to come back for the fish, but then, feeling a twinge of guilt, decides against it.

Just before the concession stand closes, Winn buys a camping permit, which allows access to the grounds, but not the lake, before the outside gates open at 6 a.m. The trio is determined to be the first on this fish the next day. But they'll have competition: Dan Barnett, 14, calls his 18-year-old brother, Steve, and they decide to come out to Dixon early the next morning to take their shot.

In retrospect, Malmstrom says he learned two things that day. "I'm never calling those meatheads ever again when I'm on a big fish," he says with a chuckle. "And I'll be sure to take the next day off from work."

Weakley, Dickerson, and Winn grew up in Escondido. They met in the fourth grade and have been best friends ever since, bonds forged tight by the anguish of broken families. In a span of two years when they were teenagers, Weakley's father died of a heart attack and both Dickerson's and Winn's parents split up. The boys escaped by spending hours trout fishing on nearby Dixon Lake.

In his 20s, Weakley began to frequent the Indian casinos that had popped up in the area, becoming a regular at the low-stakes poker tables. One day a man approached him, impressed by the clean-cut young man's knowledge of and hunger for gambling. He offered Weakley a job as a manager in his company, Pacific Gaming, which provides the betting cash for casinos in Southern California. Weakley liked the job, liked hanging out at casinos and card rooms, liked the high-risk vibe and the big money. He was good at watching the cash, and his boss told him to hire two lieutenants. Weakley hired Dickerson, who had been installing carpets, and Winn, who had been working as a first mate on a deep-sea fishing boat. The trio hung out together every day on the job and off, when they trout fished on Dixon.

At the beginning of 2001, they noticed that Mike Long, the unquestioned king of the San Diego big-bass scene, was fishing Dixon nearly every day. He seemed to be onto something, working his boat slowly along the shoreline, staring into the water, as if the lake's bottom were lined with gold. In a sense it was: That year, an outfit in Tampa called the Big Bass Record Club was offering $8 million to the angler who broke George Perry's iconic 1932 world record for largemouth bass. The three friends, ever the gamblers, liked the odds of finding that fish in their home lake, which they knew so well. They ditched their trout gear, bought heavy rods, and became bass fishermen.

Their methods were primitive at first. Plastic worms and live shiners were their bait, not the jigs and swimbaits that serious big-bass hunters preferred. Determined to learn, they approached Mike Long to pick his brain, but he spurned the upstarts. So they studied him on the water from afar and found out how to fish for big bass the hard way. That year, the trio logged more than 200 days at Dixon.

In the spring of 2001, they were bystanders as Mike Long caught a 20-pound 12-ounce bass from Dixon, the eighth largest ever at the time, and the first recorded over 20 pounds in a decade. That only made the trio fish harder, even as the Big Bass Record Club, along with its $8 million bounty, disappeared. Why they fished now wasn't because of money but something else entirely: They had become too good to stop.

In 2003, Weakley caught a 17-8, then the 19-8. Later that spring, Dickerson capped it all with the 21-11, the fish that officially put the men on the big-bass map. Long was at the lake on the day Dickerson landed that fish and claimed that it was the same one he had caught two years earlier, when it was a pound lighter. The evidence: It had the same dime-size black dot underneath its jaw. A few weeks later, Long said that some trout fishing friends had found the fish floating dead; he'd sent the carcass to a taxidermist. Weakley never believed him. "Total B.S.," he says. He suspected that Long was just trying to keep the hordes off of his honey hole, figuring that someone could catch that fish again, and this time it just might be the actual world record.

Mike Long had good reason to worry.

At 4 a.m. on March 20, Jed Dickerson flashes his camping permit and passes through the gates at Dixon. Weakley and Winn are getting doughnuts and coffee. The night before, the trio hatched their plan. Underlying their conversations was something they didn't dare verbalize: This bass could be the one.

Weakley and Winn arrive at 5 a.m. The three of them gather in Weakley's car and listen to the radio. Dazed by the early-morning hour, they barely utter a word until Weakley, pointing at the windblown streaks of rain on the car window, says, "Man, what the hell are we doing here?" They laugh, knowing the answer.

Meanwhile, Dan and Steve Barnett nudge their car up to the Dixon gate outside the grounds, but at 6 a.m., after running to the concession stand to get their permits, they glance down to the water and see Weakley, Winn, and Dickerson already in a boat. The camping permit has worked. The Barnett brothers, with no shot at the fish, opt to watch the action from the handicap dock. Chris Bozir, a part-time dock attendant, joins them.

Winn, as always, mans the motor. Weakley and Dickerson stand, rods ready. They ease toward the handicap dock. Wind and rain make it impossible to see anything more than the shadow of the fish. But she's there.

The first cast is Dickerson's. Tossing out his white Bob Sangster jig underhand, he lets it sink to the bottom and sit, a foot or two away from the fish. Then he works the lure over the nest. He jerks the rod tip, making the skirt billow and contract. The bass turns but doesn't take. Weakley then tosses in his jig. The huge female's consort, a 3-pound male, gets agitated, racing around the bed and diving on the lure.

Dickerson and Weakley continue to alternate casts. Three times, Dickerson thinks the bass bumps his lure, and he instinctively swings his rod but fails to connect. The visibility is so poor that he can't be sure if it's the male or the female that's hitting his jig. Weakley tries to set the hook a few times, too, and also comes up empty. No one—either on the boat or the dock—is talking much.

After 45 minutes, Weakley feels his line twitch again, and he swings hard. This time his rod doubles in half. Time doesn't slow down, as it's supposed to. It speeds up. The fish dives for deeper water, jerking the 15-pound-test line from his reel. She begins to give in a bit, and he reels, fast. Weakley knows that truly big bass don't fight that well. Their obscene girth tires them quickly, like a 400-pound man trying to climb stairs.

When Weakley gets the bass close to the boat, Winn reaches down with the net but misses. With new life, the bass runs hard for the handicap dock and the audience gathered there. Weakley pulls on his rod with all his strength, determined to keep her away from the pilings. He turns her head, then easily reels her in. This time, Winn gets her with one scoop.

To the Barnett brothers, this is the most exciting thing they have ever witnessed on the water. The scene has played out not 15 feet away, and now the show has reached its climax. "That's an insanely enormous bass," Steve remarks.

But then he sees something else, something that deflates his euphoria. The white jig is embedded in the fish's back, maybe 3 inches behind the dorsal fin. Steve groans and yells, "Oh man, it's foul-hooked!" Weakley and Winn glance in the direction of the yell, momentarily distracted from the black-and-silver mass of fish in the net.

Their attention quickly returns to the bass. Winn unhooks the jig and runs a stringer through the fish's mouth. Though the fight took little physical energy, the three men notice they are breathing heavily. Lying on the boat's bottom is the biggest bass that any of these men have ever seen. It's the one.

They should feel total elation, but Weakley keeps looking down at a spot on the fish's back, the hole left by the jig. I foul-hooked the damn thing, he thinks. Then he hears voices on the dock. The audience is clamoring to see the fish up close. Winn hears them, too. Reaching for the trolling motor, he instead heads for the middle of the lake after the others lower the stringer into the water. The trio talk for a few minutes, casting occasional glances at the fish tied to the boat. They lift her out of the water and put her on Dickerson's handheld Berkley scale: 25.5. The weight is far above the magical mark of 22 pounds 4 ounces. They motor back to the dock.

The moments there are chaotic and quick. They hang the fish on the scale again. Now it shows 25.1 pounds. Weakley gets out his video camera and shoots the footage of the fish that will soon appear on ESPN and various evening news shows. Toward the end of the shaky clip, the camera pans in on the fish, and a disembodied voice from somewhere behind it utters five words: "That's the beast right there."

Dickerson wants to take a photo of Weakley with the fish, but Weakley says his arm is too tired from lifting it. Winn stands in, grabbing the fish with one arm. The photo is snapped. Later that day, it would fly around the Internet, incorrectly captioned as "Mac Weakley."

Weakley and Dickerson look at the fish more closely. They notice something: a dime-size black dot under the fish's jaw. "I'm 100 percent sure that this is the same fish I caught in 2003," says Dickerson, which, of course, would make it the same fish that Mike Long caught in 2001. A replica mount from the 2003 catch was featured on the cover of *Field & Stream*. This is a bass accustomed to the limelight. Then the men notice something else: a short strand of 2-pound-test running out of the bass's mouth. Remember Six Pack, the old trout fisherman?

Then Steve Barnett hears either Weakley or Dickerson say, "Look, there's a mark on its back." He can't quite remember who uttered those words amid all the excitement. Steve is confused, not exactly sure what the comment means, what whoever said it is trying to imply. "We saw you foul-hook it, though," Steve says, pleading almost, still unsure. Then he hears Weakley tell Winn to release the fish. Winn unhooks the stringer, and the biggest bass in the world swims lazily away and disappears.

The beast? Well, that turns out to be something else entirely.

A ranger at Dixon makes a phone call to a friend, the first trickle in what will become a flood. It builds with more phone calls, then e-mails and Internet chat-room postings. Within a few hours, the first news stories hit the wires.

At first the attention is fun for the men. This is the fish they have worked so hard for, justification for the hours, days, months, and years they've been after it. "You always heard people claiming that they saw a 25-pounder," says Weakley. "We proved it exists."

Over the next two days, Weakley does dozens of interviews—*The New York Times, Los Angeles Times, Associated Press, The Early Show* on CBS. ESPN sends a camera crew to the lake. They retest Dickerson's scale with a 5-pound weight. It's perfectly accurate. News reports deem the fish the new world record, even as they note the ambiguous manner in which the fish was caught and documented. An IGFA official is quoted as saying that the foul hooking may or may not matter, and that Weakley should submit his application anyway. The one sticking point seems to be a California state regulation that says that any fish not caught in the mouth must be released immediately.

In the beginning, Weakley contemplates going against his own first impulse and sending in the photo, the videos, and the testimony of the five witnesses to the IGFA. He's buoyed by the praise, caught up in the attention.

But quickly, the murmurs of a conspiracy become shouts. People start to focus on the negative: There's the foul hooking. The fact that the fish wasn't weighed on a certified scale, even though there was one maybe 100 feet away in the ranger's office. The lack of measurements of the fish's length and girth. "These boys know the rules better than anyone and they didn't follow them," says Ray Scott, a voice to be reckoned with because of his considerable influence on the IGFA record committee.

For some, the questions become broader. What are the ethics of fishing for a spawning bass on its bed? And what about the unnaturalness of California bass, Florida transplants that are hand-fed thousands of pounds of planted rainbow trout? The attacks even get personal. These guys work in the shadowy world of gambling. What about the unsavory nature of the $1,000 offer and the camping permit?

Less than 48 hours after catching his fish, Weakley sits in his house, hollow-eyed, exhausted. Winn has been on the Internet, checking the pulse of the bass fishing nation. After agonizing over the question with Winn and Dickerson, Weakley decides he doesn't want to prolong the negativity. He goes with his initial gut instinct. He foul-hooked the fish. It shouldn't count. He won't pursue the record.

"I know we did the right thing," says Weakley. "Look, me and Buddha and Jed got to hold a 25-pound bass. No one else ever has. That was cool for us." He thinks it's all over now, but the calls still stream in at all hours of the day and night. Local newspaper writers approach him with proposals for screenplays. Eventually, he's overwhelmed and turns off his phone, done with the telling and retelling.

Meanwhile on Dixon, there's world-record hysteria. Lake ranger Jim Dayberry estimates that business is up 80 percent over normal. On many days, some 30 boats jockey for space on the tiny body of water. "And everyone coming in here says they want a shot at that bass," Dayberry says. A man flies in from Texas and rents a motor home and fishes for a week. Anglers from at least 20 different states have called asking about reservations. And amid it all, an old man sits at his normal post, fishing for trout.

The irony, of course, is that George Washington Perry's fish, the 22-pound 4-ouncer caught in the backwoods of Georgia in 1932, would have been just as controversial, if not more so, in our modern age. There's no photo of his fish and no mount. Nobody ever made contact with the only witness to the catch. Perry simply weighed his fish at a country store and sent the information to a *Field & Stream* contest. Then he took the bass home and ate it.

But Perry's story, true or not, carries incredible resonance to this day. It's a symbol of a more innocent age, of the egalitarian American ideal that any man, no matter his station in life, can achieve greatness. It's grown more powerful over the years, snowballing in the way that stories that are passed down from generation to generation tend to do. It's no coincidence that it's primarily older men who are Perry's fiercest protectors. This new era of nakedly ambitious record chasing seems to them to be blasphemous, a perversion of the right way—and the right reasons—to fish.

Months after Weakley caught his fish, the media firestorm has burned into smoldering embers, now almost gone. As he sits in his house in Carlsbad, his 8-month-old boy asleep in the next room, Weakley is finally able to reflect. And what he finds isn't that pretty. "I look back now and it all seems kind of sick," he says. "Fishing is supposed to be fun." Maybe like it was when he was a teenager and he and Winn and Dickerson would head to Dixon to blow off steam and fish for trout. He thinks about some of the stories that were written, of the excessive importance given to this record, the opinions—the real beast that emerged from the water that day.

"I see how stupid it all is. It's actually been a nice wake-up call," he says. "Me and Buddha and Jed realize now that we should get out and live life and spend more time with our families rather than being obsessed with a fish. It's just a fish. Just a stupid fish."

But that fish may be back next spring, drawn into Dixon's shallows by the urge to spawn. Rest assured, Weakley, Dickerson, and Winn will be there too, lured by the equally powerful pull of obsession.

MY TARPON ADDICTION

THOMAS MCGUANE

In the dark, not quite dark with a three-quarter moon shining overhead, I pictured myself colliding with unlighted pilings, stone crab traps or oyster bars that I couldn't see. Chains of islands both to the east and the west were just streaks in the night sky, and I hoped I would recognize my destination when I got to it. There would be a row of fishermen's shacks on an oyster reef, then an opening, then a small, hidden basin appended to a forked channel. I knew I'd see the silhouettes of the shacks but was not so sure I'd see the opening. Indeed, I overran it and only the sudden dark shapes in front of me made me know that I was about to go high and dry in a planing skiff.

By the time I shut down, I was floating in less than a foot of water. I got out my pushpole and began to work my way in the presumed direction of the basin. If, as I worried, I had fetched up on some wide shallow, I would find no tarpon today. Fish were shooting off around me, I guessed redfish, and it was interesting going but uncertainty had taken away some of the pleasure. At about the time I thought I would try a new angle, the pushpole dropped out from under me and I knew I was in the basin. I was confident that when the sun came up, I'd be in the middle of a lot of innocent tarpon.

If there were rollers, I'd see them in the moonlight or at daybreak, which was now less than an hour away. In any case, a bonanza was at hand. All I needed was a little light.

The sun came up and I poled myself into an irritable sweat before admitting that the fish were not here. I was in the wrong place at the wrong time. I suppose if you can't take this, you can't take tarpon fishing. Only the vision of things going right, of fish this big that can run this far and jump this high, keep tarpon fishermen knocking their heads against the mysteries. I had been immersed since the earliest fish showed here in South Florida in March, and despite irregular success, I could think of little else. The fuel bills were mounting and miles by the thousands were accumulating on the log of my GPS.

When I've found them in years past, the fishing has had a classic quality: laid-up fish, floating, asleep but ready to be drawn into pursuit. This is exacting, addictive fishing because the casts must be accurate and from a distance. When the cast is right, and the fish stirs to track the fly, in all his great weight and pent-up exuberance, the riveted excitement is like nothing else. This year, I couldn't find them. The fish were not in short supply in nearby water, were thick even, but they weren't coming to my hidden basin, not many anyway, not enough—though with each visit something happened that made me come back for another look. Inevitably, it was a free jumper rocketing from the water, hanging in midair before the crash that seemed to be the fish's object; or it was a fish feeding, perhaps on a mullet: an abrupt canyon in the tannic water that closed with overlapping waves gathering at the middle of a subsiding hole. Gone.

I came back that night, the next morning: I never caught them. This was a scene of subtle opportunity, and I seemed not to be up to it. At night as I drifted off, I pictured a sustained time during which I stayed in that basin, risking time, consuming failure, until the answers of tide, wind and migration were understood. Of course, if I succeeded, it would be all mine and perhaps I would be slow to share my secret.

I started the engine and idled while I thought about what to do, whereupon I received one of the gifts that come to anglers only when they fish unstintingly, especially in saltwater where the tide goes from

something you read on a chart to something in your blood; a tissue laid over the intuitions of fish movement that gets teased about by the vagaries of weather, especially winds that change water temperature or produce lees in specific places–from all of which comes the gift: a hunch.

Here was the hunch: a long grassy hump, almost black, in 4 feet of water with a round sand spot that would expose anything swimming over it. The falling tide crossed it at an acute angle and it would be an ideal checkpoint for tarpon moving on the tide to one of three passes opening to the Gulf of Mexico.

An angler ignoring his hunches discounts his opportunities. This one was strong and I followed it, a long run in a steep quartering chop that kept me in stinging spray the whole way, or at least until I entered the quieter waters of the sound. When I reached my spot, the hunch transformed itself into real conviction as I savored the light on my pass point, light which seemed to illuminate a broad area of turtle grass and the nicely defined edge. I anchored my skiff and tied the rode off with a quick-release knot, the bitter end of which was attached to an orange float.

I was not long awaiting my travelers. The first were a string of smaller fish, rolling and moving merrily a bit out of range. They were followed by singles and more strings of fish, also out of range. And just as my conviction began to weaken and I thought of moving my anchor, five big fish cut across the grass toward the edge from an entirely new angle, one less advantageous to me as it would have my fly approaching them from behind, something tarpon will not tolerate. I suspected that there might be one more fish, coming after these five. I cast just behind the last fish I could see and let my fly float until an apparition appeared, moving over the grass, and I started my retrieve. The fish moved so quickly, I never saw it. Instead, the rod jolted in my hand, the fish was running, and I was clambering to the stern to pull the slipknot on my anchor line. The first jump was a twister that had the fish landing on its back; then one marlin style with a lot of horizontal distance covered; then several more until they became diminished efforts with only the upper part of the fish's body above the surface. Still I had trouble moving it and had to go to the fish with the motor. I stopped and tried to turn the fish, which responded with shorter and shorter but still powerful surges. We had gone a long way together. Halfway across the sound, the tarpon was finning beside the boat. The lower jaw makes a good grip for removing the hook and I held on for a few more moments just to feel the weight, the remaining power.

The best part is watching them swim away, in no particular hurry. Now, to hunt up the orange float, and perhaps have my beer and ham sandwich. It was 90 degrees and I was imagining the big chunk of ice in my cooler, the lovely breeze as I ran home.

I went out to the Gulf on a hot evening to fish one tide. It was very quiet with a few swimmers on the beach in the distance and towering pink thunderheads with dark bellies over the mainland. I scared some tarpon as I maneuvered into my stakeout and was not waiting long before the first fish came along from the south, singles, pairs, strings, moving quickly. I misunderstood the speed of the first fish and they overtook me before I could present my fly and flushed from the boat in whirlpools of turbulence. The next bunch came at a bad angle to my left but I cast anyway and to my surprise the biggest fish turned out and tracked my fly for a long way, then lifted up in the deep shoveling take that no one gets accustomed to, and I hooked it. This, like most first jumps, seemed enraged, an attempt to knock me out with the first blow, then several more as violent followed by a burning run. The fight took us straight offshore in fading light, and trying to force the issue, I leaned into the 11-weight, faithful friend of over a decade, and broke it. The shattered tip traveled down the line and then the sharp edge of the broken butt cut the backing, and my fly line went over the horizon. If there is any weakness in your tackle, tarpon find out about it.

When I got home, Austin Lowder was in my living room with the battered insulated coffee cup with which guides keep their bodies in motion during tarpon season. He looked discouraged. "I had my guy in fish all day. Nice guy. But stupid. IQ around 55 but we got along great. Show him a hundred fish and he goes, 'Which one do I cast to?' He casts and I have to tell him to strip. 'Strip,' I tell him. 'STRIP! STRIP! STRIP!' It was hopeless. At the end of the day, still no fish. He asks me to tell him what he should do. I'm like, 'Dude! I can't take any more! Catch a tarpon! I recommend that you catch a tarpon.'"

My Montana friends George Anderson and Bill Hart showed up, as well as a stream of other visitors, most with beer in hand. We had line burns in the crevices of our fingers. There were bits of 80-pound fluorocarbon in the rug from building shock tippets. An argument broke out as to whether the Slim Beauty knot is as strong as the Australian plait or the Bimini twist. Everyone was thinner than they were 60 days ago. Two-stroke engines had made us half deaf. We tried to remember the last time we'd read a book or newspaper. One report said the president was flying to France to meet with a bunch of cheese-eating surrender monkeys. No other news available. The fishing guides seemed embittered that when they finally get into fish, the clients have to go back for massages or manicures. There was also some tension between the guides and us unguided "privateers."

Austin started his day at five in the morning, took a short nap at my house at midday, fished till nine at night, dropped the client, headed out to fish himself, came in at 3:30 a.m., made a peanut butter jelly sandwich in my kitchen, then picked up his client 90 minutes later for another day on the water. Some guides actually like to fish.

I felt that I really should catch up on the news: Here and there, we are advised to stay the course. Tests show that doctors' ties are full of germs. Most Americans are too busy to floss. Others have made "the ultimate sacrifice." Everything seemed so abstract, especially the pompous overviews of the talking heads. I'd lost touch and the fishing had become a parallel universe. It couldn't last, could it? Probably it shouldn't last but it seemed so real next to the streaming nightmare of the news. I could get pretty abstract myself, explaining that I was "trying to get to the bottom of this" by way of accounting for how a tarpon obsession could get so out of control for three unbroken months.

"When do you think you're coming home?" asked my wife.

"I have a ticket for Sunday," I assured her.

"Do you think you'll be on that plane?"

After a thoughtful pause, I said, "I wish I knew." I said that I was like the house cat that had been making love to a skunk.

"How's that, dear?"

"I haven't had enough but I've had all I can stand."

"Ha ha," she said mirthlessly. "I think you can stand more. Yes, I think you can stand more. Have you learned anything?"

"Yes, I've learned that you cannot live entirely on Krispy Kreme doughnuts."

"Oh."

"You must have fiber. By combining Krispy Kremes with Metamucil and black coffee, I have a complete diet."

I actually had a nice meal that evening sitting on my poling platform in the rolling Gulf, looking for fish, rod in reach. I'd laid out cold sliced pineapple, slices of Fuji apples, a big piece of Black Diamond cheddar, a wedge of cold sirloin and a green bottle of beer. Sometimes I saw a manta ray jump, or a manatee bulge to the surface, or a shoal of bait go airborne, or frigate birds sortie forth on a twilight mission, the heedless plunges of pelicans, a sail on the horizon: It was quite good. Yes, a pleasant way to dine. I had been less pleased in the twilight of famous French restaurants, with gourmands blowing cigarette smoke in my face.

Then, where the pass met the deep flat and the color changed from cobalt to foam mid-Gulf pale green, right there, a string of playful tarpon was streaming north, the late light illuminating the frolic as well as the long bar of silver when several rolled at once. It was my job to guess where they were going, to get there and shut down quietly. The line of travel was constant and I had little difficulty moving into their path and waiting. I began checking my equipment more urgently as the fish approached—checked the line, checked the loop in the water for flotsam of any kind, the fish now with separate bodies and those curiously unseeing above-the-water eyes. Every few seconds a tail kicked clear as a fish fed and they started to chain up, then straightened again and came my way. I looked once more to see if I was standing on line, and then threw my reading glasses on their lanyard around behind my back having suddenly remembered how they've snagged line and robbed me of fish before. Now I began talking to myself: They're not in range, they're not in range, please be cool. The lead fish was bigger than the others, dorsal slicing the water and pulling a quarter wave behind him as I realized suddenly how fast these fish were really going. As they bore off slightly to my left, I cast an interception, waited, then retrieved across the vision of the lead fish. Instead of taking as it crossed in front of him, the fish slowed and began to track the fly, doing so for 20 feet, until I was thinking we were within a couple of yards of the boat flushing the whole school. But the fish pushed up behind my fly, tilted, and that stupendous maw opened, and my fly went down. I continued to strip until I had contact, then using only my stripping hand, I struck the fish and tightened, reaching with my line hand as far away from my side as I could. The coils were leaping toward the stripping guide and then I was clear, and in the words of Mike Tyson, "It's on."

The first jump often seems to express the greatest fury: the olive-brown fish in the water has become the plated silver fish in the air, and his body has at least two violent curves in it as the fish seems to truly reach for the sky. The reentry is a heedless crash, then reorientation into a straightaway dash, the substantial line becoming the seemingly insubstantial backing as the run accelerates and you feel the elevation of line as another jump and another, each crazier than the last, marks several spots in the sea at once.

Why is it so thrilling? Why is it incomparably thrilling? It's the contest joined, but it's also a kind of euphoric admiration and—this is risky—it feels like love. You watch your fish and you are filled with admiration, transported by beauty—isn't that love? It was in high school!

The jumping has proved costly and the fish must now slug it out with you and you don't necessarily want to slug it out with him. Barring tackle failure, you have every chance of winning this phase but make it quick: learn every fish-fighting technique out there because love and admiration are not the same as beating up the object of your desire. I have come to feel quite ambivalent about this side of angling. I delight in seducing fish and insinuating myself into their private world; but defeating fish has less appeal, though I continue to boat tarpon from time to time, to remind us both that this is mortal combat.

By late May, a tarpon fishing death march was in play. Things began going haywire for everybody. I put a lot of pressure on a straight-running, non-jumping fish and the Dacron backing stripped the coating off my fly line at the nail knot and the line was gone with leader, fly, and fish. George Anderson reported that loose fly line jumping around the deck while a tarpon was running had caught the keys to his boat, ripped them out of the ignition, and thrown them overboard.

Most afternoons, George was napping between sessions on a rolled-up tarp in my carport. Montana log builder Bill Hart tried sleeping on the porch but, soaking with sweat, adjourned to the dock where he rested on the widely spaced planks. Austin snoozed in the guest room. Crushed ice in the coolers didn't make it through the day, and we turned to block. Three guys and a Gordon setter from West Yellowstone never came ashore. It was all part of the Montana hatch on the Gulf. My charge account at the fuel dock kept me at arm's length from reality; and we were all fingering places on our bodies to speed up the dialogue with our dermatologists.

Predawn runs were at fatalistically high rpms, and the imaginations that once conjured up hazards now only pictured the destination and its fish. Early one morning I took a jaunt with George, who believes that when it comes to a fast skiff, you should "drive it like you stole it." Indeed as we hurtled along, I took a concerned look at the GPS to get a real idea of our speed. As we whined and skittered south toward Fort Myers, I determined that we were pushing 60 and that not much of the boat was ever actually in the water. "The reason this thing is so slow," George explained, noting my alarmed gaze at the speed indicator, "is I have the wrong prop on it."

The tarpon came in pulses from the south and we watched for them like herons with the faith that our trails would cross in the land of fate. A few times when a hunch placed me in some incongruous spot, a breach in the mangroves, the corner of a tidal bore, the tarpon appeared and it was enough to think, There you are, as the fish changed direction and swam out of range. A moment of recognition between two watchful beasts.

We like to think that we "know" things and that animals are merely programmed. Tarpon know to spawn offshore and their progeny know to head inshore to the brackish mangroves to grow up safely. They know to follow migrating baitfish and they know at what stage of tide the crabs hatch. They know to go south in the spring and up rivers when it's cold, and when to return south in the fall. Some fish know their way around both coasts of Florida and the Gulf to Louisiana and Texas. They know which fish they can eat and they know which ones can eat them. They know man is a bad thing the first time they see him. They know when the palolo worm hatches and will travel for miles to arrive just when dinner is served. They know that a safe snooze can be had in the shade of a Gulfport or Key West shrimp trawler. By the time you can catch tarpon consistently, when you are convinced you know what they know, you think so much like them that your affection can create some problems.

Marshall Cutchin, an old friend from Key West, and I were fishing with George one May evening on a long, sweet, curving shoreline that seemed to be a runway for inbound tarpon traffic. The fish were assembling in loose groups, then stringing out in meandering lines, happy fish that had one thing in common: They weren't biting. We threw everything at them and they weren't even courteous enough to boil off in indignation. Each had that faraway look that is connected less to hunger than to destiny. This produces a new kind of effort from the angler: narcissistic casting based on no expectation of results. Tight loops! Casts so long no hook could be set. And so on and so forth. Another string of travelers came by, all average fish; I cast and from the shadows beneath the string a very different fish arose and wolfed my fly. I set the hook and the fish jumped with magnificent hang time. "That's a big fish," George stated. Marshall said, "Tom, that's an awful big fish." The hook was firmly set, the fish began that run characteristic of big tarpon—reminiscent of expensive German automobiles—and ping! The reel froze. The three of us looked into the arbor of the reel. I was sad and shaken.

"What was that all about?"

"What happened?"

"Could I have done something?"

"A trapped loop?"

"I wish I was dead."

"There'll be more."

"Like that?"

"Well..."

"Like that?"

I knew I'd do well to get a grip on myself.

MY TARPON ADDICTION

Once June came around it was hot before the sun came up. Standing on the deck fueling my skiff, I could watch my sweat rain around my feet. As I idled out of the canal, my eyes went to patches of shade and not to the glare of the Gulf beyond. Instead of thinking how many trout it would take to make a meal for a tarpon, I began to think how beautiful a trout looks when it tips up under a mayfly. And what about a nice cow in a green meadow? I began to believe that the tropics make man forget reading, writing and arithmetic; and my checkbook confirmed this point. How clever folks are in the north, I marveled. Shutting down whole wings of the hotel was grimly logical; the rapidly decaying local civility gave rise to an ill-tempered poetry as angry folks tried to communicate. At the store, the oranges were from California, the mangoes from Brazil and the berries from Chile. The bag boy, 80, was from Yonkers and the checkout clerk, Cleveland. The entire island was covered with evil green rapidly growing plants advancing on seasonal homes with ill-concealed malice.

I hooked a hot fish on the edge of the Intercoastal Waterway. When it went airborne, a Cigarette boat full of bathing beauties stopped to watch but left in a roar when the tarpon stopped jumping. Then I was alone with the fish, which, after two long straight runs, let me bring it slowly to the boat. My arms were dead. I hung over the gunwale and removed the fly, then held the great fish by its lower jaw. I could see every detail of its iridescent shape in the pellucid green water, turtle grass and seashells a few feet below. I could feel the slow beat of its tail all the way up through my shoulder, even into my body; I could see the curls of water driven by its lazy power. I hung low over the side of the boat until I looked into those huge black eyes. I said, "I gotta go." I knew I'd make that plane. I opened my hand and all the migratory wisdom in that gaze faded to green and the fish was gone.

RED, WHITE, AND BLUEGILL

TED LEESON

Among angling aristocrats, Atlantic salmon have long been celebrated as "the fish of kings," no doubt because the two have so much in common: the aloof arrogance and inflated sense of self-worth, a fussiness about habitat, expensive tastes. And as far as I'm concerned, they deserve each other. Give me a panfish any day—a fish of the people, blue-collar rather than blue blood, a working-class fish, a fish for a great republic. I've never understood how the bald eagle, a scavenger and a thief, could have been chosen as our national symbol, whereas the honest, sweat-of-the-brow bluegill never even made the shortlist. I guess the Founding Fathers didn't fish much.

Panfish, of course, doesn't denote a particular species but a loosely defined assemblage with varying regional representatives—a little like Congress but harder working and better behaved. The core of the group comes from the Centrarchidae family—the sunfishes—itself a kind of melting pot whose chief ingredients include bluegills, pumpkinseeds, redears, redbreasts, green sunfish, warmouths, rock bass, and white and black crappies. A kind of odd-man-out, the yellow perch is not a sunfish but no less a panfish wherever it is found. I'm not aware of any single place that's home to all these species at once. They crop up in various mixes and proportions in different geographical areas, and membership in the category of panfish (or "bream" or "brim," depending on where you live) has always been a matter of shifting local interpretations, further complicated by a host of colloquial names: shellcracker, stumpknocker, goggle-eye, sun perch, longear, speckled perch, white bass, and so on. In practice, the term ultimately falls into that set of expressions, like "I'll do it in a minute" or "I have strong feelings for you," that are universally understood but not necessarily taken to mean exactly the same thing by everyone.

Fishermen don't trouble themselves much about such discrepancies, instead focusing on the collective virtues of the fish. And foremost among their merits is a relentless availability. Like the other indispensables of American life—duct tape, canned chili, and WD-40—panfish can be obtained virtually everywhere. I've taken them in creeks and rivers, brackish water and fresh, 10,000-acre lakes and quarter-acre stock tanks, old quarry pits, prairie potholes, golf-course water hazards, abandoned strip mines, backyard ponds, irrigation ditches, and once, the ornamental fountain pool behind a fancy hotel. As a group, they are America's most widespread and abundant gamefish. And they are nothing if not game. I've caught them by accident and on purpose, on handlines, trotlines, poles cut from tree limbs, garage-sale spincast outfits, fly tackle that cost slightly less than my car, and every kind of gear in between. I've grabbled a few by hand and (in a mercifully brief period of angling dementia) jigged them up through 2 feet of ice. Equally ready for a few casual casts after work or the formalities of an organized expedition, panfish are a fish-of-all-trades, up for anything, anytime. They are a welcome counterweight to the forces of high-tech angling and a persistent reminder that fishing is finally about fish, not equipment.

Accommodating and enthusiastic, genial and cooperative, panfish are custom-cut for the neophyte. In the angling universe of my youth, they were the force of gravity that held everything together. The ones I could catch whetted my skills and honed my instincts. Those that proved better at being fish than I did at being a fisherman gave me a continuing sense of purpose. Without panfish, I might well have sunk into juvenile delinquency, or golf. The pinnacle of every summer was the day my father, a man who

did not readily leave the house, squeezed our whole family into a station wagon and endured the eight-hour drive to a lake in northern Wisconsin. He herded us directly from the car into a rowboat where, except for a few moments stolen to dig more worms, we spent a week or two yarding in unimaginable numbers of perch and rock bass and bluegills. The little ones bit readily. And the bigger ones proved just discriminating enough to teach you something but still catchable enough that you could learn the lesson. At a time of life as yet uncorrupted by a lust for magazine-cover specimens, panfish fulfilled the greatest promise in all of angling—pure action.

We ate them too, by the stringerful, with butter and lemon and onions, fried, baked, broiled, and grilled, and best of all, without guilt. Even today, in a time when quality angling for high-profile species increasingly hinges on catch-and-release, you can still sit down to a plate of bluegills or crappies without the slightest twinge of conscience or the fear of a second-rate meal. They come by their name honestly, for a pan is the highest destiny of these sweet-eating fishes. Bony? Sure, a little. And a steamed crab is mostly shell. Who's that going to stop?

Once you've got panfish in your soul, they never really leave. Not many seasons ago, a friend and I extorted an invitation to a pay-to-play trophy trout lake in the high desert of eastern Washington. The morning's fishing, though not fast, produced some remarkable trout, among the biggest of my life. Noon found us prospecting the lower end of the lake. Approaching deeper water near an earthen dam, we suddenly doubled up—smaller fish, it was clear, but dogged and determined fighters. To our utter disbelief, they turned out to be a pair of identical yellow perch a full pound apiece, with deep blue-green backs and lemon-lime flanks that shaded into fat, cantaloupe bellies. With no real idea how they got there, but a pretty good one about how to get them out, we burned up half a box of trout flies and a whole afternoon happily catching perch in a $200-a-day lake where a 5-pound rainbow scarcely elicits a yawn. That evening when our host, proud of his fishery and eager for a report, asked how we'd done, we just told him, "Couldn't have been better."

And we meant it. In this age of scientific fisheries control, of measurements and projections that produce finely calibrated angling regulations, panfish may well be the last unmanaged gamefish in America, left to themselves, on their own as they've always been and doing just fine, thank you. It's ironic that a whole sector of the fishing industry now thrives on whisking anglers off for remote and pristine destinations to experience sport of unspoiled abundance, fishing "the way it used to be." Any 8-year-old kid with a cane pole, a bike, and panfish in his heart can lead you to just such a place.

And maybe that's what I like best about them: Panfish are the most democratic of gamefish. They do not care who fishes them and bite equally for everyone. They're unimpressed by the cost of your tackle, indifferent to the methods you use, unconcerned about the bait you favor, and sometimes, whether there's any bait at all. Panfish are angling's version of the single-shot .22—sturdy and dependable, workmanlike and unpretentious. If panfish formed a baseball team, they'd be the Cubs; if you could play them on a jukebox, they'd be Hank Williams tunes; if panfish were a beer, they'd be whatever's on sale.

Oh, and there's one last thing. Except for the more cosmopolitan perch, panfish are pure homegrown. Though, like much in American life, they've been exported around the world, panfish are indigenous only to North America, native to no other part of the globe. So picture this for a moment—a red-and-white bobber twitching above the slab of a sunset-colored bluegill. Now there's something worth printing on the back of a dollar bill.

SALMON FEVER

PHIL CAPUTO

Lomand Patey is a spare man with a sunburnt face and a Newfoundland accent so thick it is, for all practical purposes, a foreign language. He doesn't say much on the long boat ride from Skinner's camp, but when he does, I have to ask him to repeat himself two or three times before I can pluck a recognizable word out of the verbal gumbo. He probably thinks I'm either deaf or stupid.

Patey has been guiding on the Big River, in northern Labrador, for 40 of his 61 years, and is said to have every rock, shoal, and sandbar charted in his head. Watching him pilot the Gander Bay riverboat around, through, and over those hazards, I believe it. The Big River is one of the premier salmon streams in North America, but our destination is a smaller waterway, Rattling Brook. Two of my fishing companions, Steve Pomezi and his son, Steve Jr., returned from there yesterday with tales of torpedo-size salmon, six of which Steve *fils* hooked and lost, while Steve *père* caught and released three times that many grilse. I'm a sucker for fish stories, the sort of guy who, in the 19th century, would have run all over the West, chasing rumors of gold strikes. In this case, I'm chasing silver, silver salmon. In four days of hard fishing, I've caught grilse and some hefty sea-run brook trout. I've raised some adult salmon but so far haven't caught one.

And so, leaving my partner, Joe Sproviero, and our guide, Eric Cranston, to fish our assigned beat near the camp, I journey downriver with Patey in quest of a trophy. In its lower reaches, the Big River is about a quarter of a mile from bank to willow-choked bank, and so shallow it sometimes seems as though a pane of glass lies between us and the bottom. Low, granite-crowned hills rise on both sides, covered in dense spruce forest. Labrador is the wildest place I've been outside of Alaska. I'm sure it has more trees than the Milky Way has stars, the vast boreal woods broken by muskeg bogs, ponds, lakes, and meadows of caribou lichen as white as sand. Wolf and bear tracks print the mud at the edges of its many rivers. Only the day before, Cranston and I saw a big black bear amble down to the rocky bank to watch Sproviero casting into a riffle. Presumably, it hoped he would hook up so it could rob him of his prize.

Patey jerks the outboard out of the water, and with the prop beating a froth, we skim over a gravel bar. I become aware of an openness in the sky ahead, and in a few minutes, the Labrador Sea spreads out before us, a cold, blue-green expanse speckled with islands. The ebbing tide leaves us just enough water to get over a flat. Labrador's population density being only a little greater than the moon's, I'm surprised, and dismayed, to see a boat hauled up onshore, near the mouth of Rattling Brook; and still more dismayed by the sight of an angler casting a spinning lure into pools I had planned to fish. After we land the boat, I decide to try the stretches upstream, hoping he hasn't disturbed them. There I find his partner bombing the runs and riffles with more hardware, which has the effect of chucking grenades on the wary salmon. A fly rod lies on the ground near the fisherman; evidently it hadn't been effective. I don't want to come off as a snobby purist, so I cheerfully ask how he's doing.

"Lots of them in there but couldn't get a rise outta one," he replies, motioning at the fly rod. "So I thought I'd try this." He shakes his head to indicate that he hasn't been any more successful with spinning tackle. He looks at me, 8-weight Sage in hand, decked out in Orvis and Cabela's regalia, and asks if I would mind if he tags along to see "how a real expert does it."

This is only the third time I've been Atlantic salmon fishing in my life, and I haven't exactly covered myself in glory. "Dude, you'd be following the wrong guy," I say, laughing.

Patey and I continue upstream, crawling over boulders and knife-edge slabs of granite. A short distance on, we climb to the top of a ledge that's 20-odd feet above Rattling Brook and downstream of a waterfall. Another ledge rises on the other side, forming a miniature gorge no more than 10 yards across. Patey says something that requires a translator, but I gather from his gestures that I should ease my way out onto the ledge and look down into the long pool below the waterfall. This I do, gingerly, because the slanty ledge is worn smooth and dampened by mist from the falls. Below, in the clear, sunlit, brandy-colored water above the tailout, is a sight to cause cardiac arrest in an angler: Half a dozen big salmon, finning in the swift current, hug the bottom between the ledge and a sizable boulder in the middle of the stream. The smallest looks to be about 10 pounds, the largest more than twice that. They're lined up like a squad of soldiers, waiting for some mysterious signal to send them up over the falls to spawn. Then I see three or four more on the far side of the boulder, and still more in the next pool down. Patey instructs me to use a weighted fly. I have only one, a conehead Woolly Bugger on loan from Pomezi Sr.

This is going to be some tricky, technical fishing, even a little dangerous. I am, in effect, perched on a slightly pitched roof slick as wet marble. Kneeling on both knees to keep myself from falling, I tie the Woolly Bugger to a long leader, strip off some line, and drop it straight down, like a kid fishing with a cane pole. The current is so fast that I'd need a Danforth anchor to keep the fly under the surface. I watch it streak over the first six fish, strip in, and, to help sink it, make a short cast upstream, toward the head of the pool. The hydraulics are a study in chaos theory—all kinds of swirls and whirlpools and eddies. The fly spins out of control, and it's all but impossible to keep a tight line.

It is said that the Atlantic salmon is the fish of 1,000 casts. I make close to 50 from various angles, and the salmon react to each presentation as Christie Brinkley would to my offer to buy her a drink. Then, as the Woolly Bugger tumbles in the deep water a few yards down from the falls, a shadow looms up from the bottom. My breath catches as a huge salmon materializes, swipes at the fly, misses it and dives, its tail breaking the surface just before it vanishes into the depths. It looks like a small tarpon, possibly 35 to 40 pounds, and it actually scares me. Fighting a fish that size in a narrow gorge, from the top of a high ledge, seems a little crazy. That is, I could easily slip and wind up in the water with it. I might drown.

But then, the Atlantic salmon tends to drive anglers crazy. It has been the prize of prizes to flyfishermen ever since Izaak Walton crowned it "the king of fresh-water fish" in his 1653 treatise, *The Compleat Angler*. I speak here of wild salmon, which are to the farm-raised variety sold in supermarkets as elk are to dairy cows. They are splendid-looking creatures, streamlined and silver, as ferocious as they are beautiful. Regrettably, they are also rare. Dams flung across their traditional migratory rivers, decades of overfishing, and other natural or man-made factors have drastically depleted wild salmon stocks throughout eastern North America, Iceland, and western Europe.

The good news is that they are making a comeback (albeit a slow one), thanks to conservation efforts sponsored by organizations such as the Atlantic Salmon Federation. In Maine's Penobscot River, considered the anchor river for salmon populations in the U.S., returns have more than doubled in the past year, from 940 fish to about 2,000. With the decline of industrialized fishing, salmon numbers in the Canadian Maritimes are on the rise. Biologists estimate that about 50,000 salmon now return to New Brunswick's Miramichi river system each year. Still, that's a tiny fraction of the vast populations that swam up the river in the distant past. In the 17th century, explorers camped along the Miramichi reported that they were unable to sleep because of the noise made by salmon crashing into the water. (Their scientific name, *Salmo salar*, means "leaping salmon.")

The mystery of their epic migrations adds to their allure. They are hatched in freshwater rivers, where they spend from one to four years, depending on location. They go through four developmental stages in their freshwater lives, from alevin to fry to parr to smolt. As smolt, they are ready to begin their 1,000-mile journeys to the sea. There, in the icy waters off western Greenland, they grow rapidly into a fifth stage, grilse. If they survive predation by humans, sharks, seabirds, and seals, they then return to their natal streams to spawn in almost exactly the same pool where they were born. No one knows how they do this. It's a feat of navigation that the most finely calibrated GPS cannot match. Fisheries biologists suspect salmon use the sun and Earth's magnetic field to chart a course back to the coasts; then local currents and specific odors, imprinted on their memories, guide them home.

Unlike Pacific salmon, which die after spawning, Atlantic salmon live to mate another day. During this phase, they grow into adults. In other words, the huge fish I see in Rattling Brook are survivalists of the first rank, the fittest of the fit.

In pursuit of *Salmo salar*, seven other New Englanders and I made a journey that didn't qualify as epic but was long enough. After an overnight in Boston, we flew to Halifax, Nova Scotia, then on to Goose Bay, Labrador, where we spent another night before boarding a floatplane to Bob Skinner's Big River Camps. It was the pilot's first flight to the camp, and he almost aborted the landing, circling six times before he brought the Twin Otter down onto a wide spot in the river. We were all a bit queasy by the time he taxied the plane to the dock. The camp, named for the man who built it in the 1960s, sat in the middle of a wilderness 100 miles from the nearest Inuit settlement. The lodge, which consisted of a log-and-frame building painted barn red, was rough but comfortable, with four two-man rooms leading off from a large dining room and lounge. After settling in, we were paired up with our guides—Sproviero and I with Cranston, the Pomezis with Patey. Bob Reichart and Tom Lloyd were assigned to Woody Elsworth; George Nemeth and Wayne Ranhosky to Jerry Connolly. Connolly's daughter, Diane Browning, was camp cook and a guide in her own right. She later told us, with a sly grin, that she was a genuine Indian princess, being descended through her father's side from one Matthew Mitchell, a legendary Micmac guide, hunter, and explorer.

Our first full day brought ideal salmon weather—overcast, with a chilly drizzle. Cranston led Sproviero and me to our beat, a fast, narrow run between the north bank of the river and an island. Salmon were flinging themselves into the air, some big enough to make my heart leap with them. Cranston showed us how to tie a riffling hitch. First, the fly is tied to the tippet with a standard improved clinch knot; then two half hitches are looped over the head of the fly and pulled tight, so the leader extends at a right angle to the shank. This causes the fly to wake on the surface, simulating a crippled baitfish trying to right itself. The struggling action deceives a salmon into thinking that an easy meal is at hand, something of a necessity because migrating salmon are more interested in getting upriver to spawn than they are in eating.

Sproviero began at the top of the run, I in the middle. Working my way downstream with short casts, mending the line to keep it taut, I drew even with a rock a few yards above the tailout. As the fly—a No. 6 Undertaker—swept past the near side of the rock, I saw a boil, felt a sudden, thrilling tug, and set the hook. The rod bowed, the shuddering line cut through the water with a prolonged hiss, and I was soon into my backing. A moment later, what looked like a chrome ingot shot skyward, flipped over, and splashed down. The salmon, a grilse of 5 or 6 pounds, made two more acrobatic jumps before it shot downcurrent. I have caught similar-size bonefish, and the strongest of them was wimpish compared with this grilse. Ten minutes later, I landed and released it, and soon beached two more, which I also let go. Later, I brought in a fine sea-run brook trout. Brookies in Labrador are almost freakishly huge—mine, a 3-pounder, was considered undersize.

Anyone observing our first full day of fishing would have had a hard time making a case that the Atlantic salmon is an imperiled species. Rotating beats, fishing three hours after breakfast, two after lunch, and two more after dinner, we caught 78 salmon and four hefty trout. All but a few were released. The elder Pomezi, a salmon master, caught the largest—12 pounds—and Nemeth took second place with a 10-pound fish. The champion in overall numbers was Pomezi Jr., who landed 18.

If I were to hand out medals for athletic angling, however, I would have to award the gold to Sproviero. This occurred on the fourth day, by which time the weather had turned fair, that is, foul, the warm, bright skies being to salmon fishing what dead air is to a sailor. As the temperature rose, our catch rate fell. Mine had plummeted to zero. Sproviero and I decided that a change of scenery would bring a change of luck, so we and Cranston tramped a mile and a half upstream to a beat the guides called the Bathtub. It had to be one of the prettiest places I have ever fished. Standing on a building-size slab of granite, we looked down into two deep pools, brown as maple syrup, one directly in front of the slab, the other on its left side, both spilling through a natural sluiceway and down a ladder-rapids into a third pool as wide as a small lake. The fast water sparkled in the sunlight, and all around spruce trees rose in dark green spires.

To complement the change in geography, I had switched tackle, swapping my graphite Sage for a rod with a history, a 40-year-old split-bamboo 9-weight that my father had bought for me in 1968, to reward me for coming home from Vietnam alive and intact. I had caught many big trout with it, plus a 10-pound salmon in western Ireland in 1974. Cranston sent me to the pool on the left, Sproviero to the other. On my second or third cast, a brook trout that must have gone 5 or 6 pounds struck my streamer and almost immediately threw the hook. A few more tosses and I had another one on. Fighting it on that old rod was a delight; the bamboo quivered as if it were alive, somehow communicating the vigor of the fish in a way that synthetics like graphite cannot. Canadian regulations allowed each angler to take home 10 pounds of trout, and having been a good, God-fearing sportsman for the previous three days, releasing everything I'd caught, I gave myself permission to kill that one. It weighed 4 pounds. "Average," said Cranston.

A moment later, a flash appeared under Sproviero's fly. His rod bent and the line slashed across the pool. At first, we thought it was a big brookie; then a huge female salmon exploded from the surface like a miniature missile. For several minutes, the fish zigged and zagged and leaped, her bright, black-spotted flanks like speckled mirrors in the sun. It appeared that he was going to land her, but she suddenly turned and streaked through the spillway and down into the rapids with astonishing speed, the reel whining. Rod in one hand, wading stick in the other, Sproviero followed, hopping along the rocky bank, scaling boulders, scrambling down, all the while keeping the line taut. She ran for close to 100 yards before stopping amid a jumble of rocks below the rapids. In effect, Sproviero was snagged. He quickly waded through the white water and crawled up a ledge, throwing slack into the line to trick the salmon into thinking she was free. The deception worked. The fish swam out of the trap, and when he reeled up the slack and she felt the hook still in her jaw, she took off on another blistering run. It looked as though she was headed for the ocean, 15 miles away. With the reel deep into the backing, he sprinted after her. If there is such a sport as Extreme Fishing, he was providing an example of it. "No way was I going to lose that fish if I could help it," he said later. But there were things he could not help. In a microsecond, his U-shaped rod straightened; the leader, abraded by the rocks, had broken, and I imagine his heart did, too.

The battle was reenacted that night over dinner, with all the appropriate hand movements. Sproviero looked like a fighter pilot, describing a dogfight.

Which brings me back to my own attempt at Extreme Fishing from atop the cliff overlooking Rattling Brook. Trying to induce the 40-pound leviathan to take another swipe at my Woolly Bugger, I make an overzealous cast across stream and hook the ledge on the opposite bank, from which there is no dislodging it. I break it off. For the next hour, I float various surface flies—Blue Charms, Undertakers, Silver Doctors, Black Bear Green Butts—over the waterfall pool, but do not draw the Beast From 20,000 Fathoms out of hiding. Nor do I attract the attention of its smaller cousins at the tailout. At one point, I knee-walk to the lip of the ledge, where, afraid of falling in, I lie down and fish on my stomach. The current carries the fly out of sight.

That's when the line tightens. I flick the rod to set the hook, and to my shock, feel the solid pull of a strong fish. This isn't Extreme Fishing; it's Extremely Ridiculous Fishing. There I am, flat on my belly, hooked to a salmon a sheer, 20-foot drop below. Somehow, I snake backward about a yard, find fairly safe footing, and stand up. The salmon jumps just then, another female, and she looks like a block of platinum infused with life, vibrant and powerful. She bolts for the falls, as if she intends to shoot right on up the cascade of roaring water, then turns, runs the length of the pool, and jumps again.

Two problems: How do I land a fish in a gorge? And where's my guide? Patey has vanished.

"Lomand! I'm on! I'm hooked up!"

He appears, no, materializes as the salmon leaps a third time, water droplets flying off her like bits of broken glass.

"Gotyeagooduntheah," says Patey, drily. "Twel', no, fideenpoun'."

The fight becomes almost a reprise of Sproviero's experience. The fish runs up and down the pool as if she's caught in a cage. Any moment now, she's going to make a break for it. Downstream, the ledge slopes off to a line of boulders. I'll be able to fight and land her there. On my rear end, I work my way down, clinging to willow clumps with one hand.

"Doanchyefallin noaow," Patey cautions.

"I am trying like hell not to!"

Inside, I'm trembling like the rod. I sense that this will be my only chance to avoid becoming The Only Guy Who Did Not Catch a Grown-Up Salmon, as tomorrow will be the last day of fishing. I manage to get off the ledge. In the lower pool, the fish repeats her performance of zipping back and forth, and also executes two spectacular jumps, turning end over end on one. Below the pool is a riffle, then another pool; below that, the stream pours like a firehose through a notch in the rocks. I stumble along, trying to get past the notch; otherwise, when the salmon bolts for open water, the leader will scrape against the rocks and part, just as Sproviero's had.

Which is exactly what happens. The fish flies out of the water and sprints away, but I'm not disappointed when the line goes suddenly, sickeningly slack. No, I'm clinically depressed. It's only later, on the fishless journey back to camp, that I'm able to snap out of my gloom. That wonderful salmon hadn't earned her freedom, for she never was indentured to me. She had merely taken back what was hers by right.

LIFE, DEATH, AND STEELHEAD

COLIN KEARNS

He eased the drift boat into the awakening river. A chinook crashed the surface. Chukars on the far bank started to cackle. The rising sun gradually lightened Mack's Canyon and opened color in the water that had streamed black in the predawn. The current carried us to the first bend, and Joe Randolph angled the oars for the turn where the Deschutes widened before us, wild and swift. The river pulsed beneath the hull. It was like riding an angry animal, sprung from its cage.

"How's your wading?" Randolph asked.

"Not bad," I said.

"O.K." He steered toward the left bank where I'd first wade across the river's dangerously slick rocks. "I'm gonna kill you right off the bat."

JEFF

Before Jeff Perin took a chance on Randolph and hired him as a steelhead guide; before Randolph, almost out of nowhere, ascended to become one of the best in the country; before their arguments about money, their falling out, and the lies and theft that followed; before Perin turned Randolph in to the police; before Randolph, 49, walked out of a bar and drove alone into the woods one night last November, the garden hose he'd stolen from Perin stashed in the back of his vehicle; before any of this, Jeff Perin and Joe Randolph were good friends.

They met in 2005, the year Randolph moved to Sisters, Ore. Randolph became a regular at the Fly Fisher's Place, a great little shop in town that Perin owns. Randolph would strut in, wearing his flip-flops, board shorts, a faded T-shirt, and that beat-up Patagonia hat, and make his way to the fly case where he'd bullshit with anyone around. Perin always loved having Randolph around the shop. He thought Randolph was a super nice guy and so easy to get along with. Before long, the two were fishing buddies.

Randolph's talent on the water stunned Perin, and every time out he only seemed to get better. Plus, he thought Randolph was a blast to fish with. Knowing Randolph didn't have a job, Perin couldn't help but imagine what a great guide he'd make. In 2007, Randolph started his career as a guide for the Fly Fisher's Place.

*****

I traveled to Oregon in Sept. 2011 to chase steelhead—a fish I'd dreamed of catching since I was a teenager, ever since I heard the sound of its superhero name. I'd booked a two-day trip on the Deschutes River through the Fly Fisher's Place, and I was told that my guide Joe wanted me to meet him at a hotel parking lot in Maupin, a town 90 miles north of Sisters, at 4:30 a.m. Afraid I'd oversleep, I pulled into the lot around 10:30 p.m. the night before and planned to sleep in my car. Little did I know there'd be an outdoor wedding reception at the hotel that would go to damn near 1 a.m. A deejay with a fondness for Def Leppard and Journey and a dance floor of hammered guests kept me up the whole time.

The next morning, right on time, I watched a pair of headlights come down the dark road and turn into the hotel lot. The vehicle stopped about 20 yards in front of me. The headlights were blasting, so I couldn't get a look at who was behind the wheel. The door opened, and a dark silhouette of a tall figure climbed out and swung the door shut. The shadow looked at me for a moment.

"Colin?"

Somehow Randolph looked more tired than I felt. This made sense when, as we crawled along the gravel road to the put-in at Mack's Canyon in Randolph's red Chevy, he mentioned that he and a friend had crashed last night's wedding and kept things going afterward. He laughed when I told him that he was the reason I couldn't sleep. As we neared the launch, Randolph asked if I'd ever caught a steelhead. "No," I said. "Always wanted to, though."

Then he asked if I'd ever cast a Spey rod, and I told him that would be a first, too. He smiled and nodded, as if realizing how difficult his job for the next two days would be. He assured me that he could help with the casting part, but what he needed most from me only I could control. "I need you to be determined that there's a steelhead on whatever rock you're casting to," he said. "You have to believe there's a fish."

FLORENCE

They met on a blind date in Monterey, Calif., in 2002. Florence Belmondo was shy back then, but Randolph made her feel comfortable right from the start. He was outgoing, charming, and fun. He took her dancing that night. About a year later, with no one else present but a judge, they got married on the beach.

As a couple, they rode quarter horses through the Carmel Valley. They traveled south to Mexico where he surfed and she boogie-boarded and ventured north to Oregon where he snowboarded and she skied—and they both fell in love with the place.

They loved how quiet and less crowded Oregon was compared with California and how much farther money could go toward a home. Randolph especially loved all the rivers, streams, and lakes; he used to tell Florence about how much he enjoyed fishing as a kid, but work, family, and life in general had made it hard for him to find time to fish as an adult. The idea of starting over again in Oregon thrilled him.

They bought a house in Sisters, and after they settled in, Florence surprised her husband with a guided fishing trip on the Deschutes. He was never quite the same after he caught his first steelhead in that river. Florence remembers he came home rejuvenated, almost like a new man. "He fell in love with flyfishing," she says.

Florence and Randolph had both been married and divorced and had children from their previous marriages. Her kids moved with them to Oregon from the start, and Randolph's—his son, Hank, and little girl, Maddi—arrived after one year, in 2006. Florence remembers how terribly Randolph missed his kids and how ecstatic he was to have them again.

As a family, they lived on a big ranch with horses and dogs and plenty of space for kids to be kids. Randolph coached the children's baseball and basketball teams while Florence cheered from the stands. As if life wasn't good enough, Randolph now lived near more water than he could fish in a lifetime.

*****

Randolph lit a Marlboro and stepped out of the anchored drift boat, clenching a 13-foot 3-inch Spey rod. He waded into the river and stopped maybe 15 paces from the bank and pushed up his fleece sleeves. His forearms were chiseled and deeply tanned, and on his inside left arm was the tattoo of a Freight Train—his favorite steelhead fly—drawn so the hook pierced his skin. As he stripped line off the reel, he walked me through the basics of Spey casting, though I didn't absorb much. I was too busy trying to keep my footing on the slick rocks, and once he started casting I was too struck to hear a word he said.

He pointed the rod tip downstream and, with energy from the current, loaded the rod and manipulated the line into graceful loops, arcs, and shoots, launching a Green Butt Skunk a mile until it landed with the gentlest drop. Even the sounds his casts made—the air whooshes and water streaks—seemed natural. He made a dozen casts, each more impressive than the last, before he handed me the rod.

"Your turn."

BRENDA

Her voice is tender as she tries hard to remember moments together with her only son. She hadn't known him in a very long time.

She remembers he was born Nov. 28, 1963, in the same New Orleans hospital where she was born. She remembers how outgoing Joey always was as a little boy, greeting folks he passed as he walked down the street.

She remembers taking Joey to fish in the park where he'd bring biscuit

dough for bait. She remembers times when Joey would be fishing with friends and he was the only one to catch anything.

She remembers one big bass that Joe caught when he was in high school, having it mounted for him, and how proud he was to hang it inside his bedroom. She remembers when Joe worked as a gas-station attendant and his boss would sometimes call asking why he never showed up for his shift. She remembers thinking, Well, he's probably gone fishing.

KAY

He was the middle child. His big sister, Kay, had come before him by about 13 months; his little sister, Fran, was three years younger. Their parents divorced when Joey was in fourth grade, and all three kids stayed with their father at first. He was a Navy pilot, and they lived at Naval Air Station Lemoore, south of Fresno, Calif.

Kay and Joey were close as kids and spent a lot of time outside. They built tumbleweed forts and declared tennis-ball-cannon wars on the neighbor kids. They dug trenches and filled them with water or fire, then made "Evel Knievel jumps" over them on their bikes. One of them always seemed to be in trouble, and when their mom or dad didn't know whom to blame, they'd blame the both of them, because they knew Kay and Joey would never tell on each other.

The kids moved around a lot, mainly up and down California, including time in Fresno with their mother. When Joey was in junior high, he and his sisters moved to Mississippi with their father and stepmom. He and Kay grew apart during that period. Sure, they'd gone their separate ways, as siblings at that age often do—but Joey had changed, Kay remembers. He would get angry and act hostile, particularly toward his stepmom. "He wasn't nice to her," Kay says, matter-of-factly. His behavior reached the point where it was best for everyone if he moved back to Fresno to live with his mother.

About a year later, Kay also moved back to California to attend Fresno State. Maybe it was the time apart, maybe they just missed being friends. Whatever the reason, Kay and her brother became close again. He was in high school—old enough to go by "Joe" now, but still too young for a driver's license, so Kay was his ride to the river. She'd help him load the flat-bottomed boat he'd built himself from plywood and fiberglass into the back of her small pickup. "I need to get out there on the water," he told her. "Fishing on the shore isn't good enough."

She'd drop her brother off at the San Joaquin River or Millerton Lake and a few hours later, when Joe came off the water, she was there to bring him home.

*****

I can hold my own with a fly rod and I assumed that skill would transfer to a Spey rod. I was wrong. At the first few holes, I was a disaster. Every other cast, it seemed like the fly either smacked the rod blank and died midcast or snagged the bank behind me. Time after time, Randolph had to untangle my line or retie my rig entirely. He never put me down, but I could tell that he was getting frustrated. What good is it to race to the best water first if you can't even make a decent cast?

I'd only known Randolph for a few hours but already I liked him. I admired his talent with such an intricate skill and sensed that any frustration he might've felt did not stem from impatience with me. He'd be there to help me all day long. But he needed me to get better at Spey casting, because until I did he couldn't help me catch my first steelhead—a fish that I was beginning to believe Randolph wanted as badly as I did. For the rest of the time we spent at that pool, I erased the idea of catching a fish just yet. Instead, I focused only on the casting—the motion, the timing, the rhythm—so I'd be ready for the next spot.

JEFF

After Jeff Perin hired him as a guide, Randolph would go fishing alone, for days at a time, to master the rivers and creeks of central Oregon. Randolph discovered the best holes, figured out how to run the roughest rapids, and waded boulder to boulder till he found that magic drift. He taught himself skills with a Spey rod that took other anglers seasons to master. "He'd go practice, practice, and practice until he perfected it," Perin says. "He absorbed everything. Joe was one of the best steelhead fishermen I had ever seen—certainly the best steelhead guide I'd ever worked with—and it didn't take him much time to get to where he was."

As to how Randolph became so good so fast, Perin has a few ideas: For starters, the guy was a natural athlete. Randolph, who went to junior college on a basketball scholarship, stood 6-foot-5 and could easily wade the deeper holes where steelhead often hold. A former surfer and scuba diver, he was fearless in water—an advantage in a river as dangerous as the Deschutes. In his 30s, while living in northern California, Randolph had taught himself golf and become great enough to work as a pro at one of the world's most famous clubs, Pebble Beach. The rhythm and power of his golf swing translated into a fluid and far-reaching Spey cast, one of the most beautiful Perin has ever seen.

Randolph fished by a maxim that Perin came up with on a trip down the Deschutes: Wade deep. Cast far. Fear not. Randolph understood as well as anyone that steelheading demands determination. Determination to get up before dawn to reach the best spot first. To meet dangerous waters head on. To make one more cast, then one more, then one more . . . and never stop, because that determination fuels an unconditional belief that on every single cast a steelhead is going to strike. "Eventually, I can give up on steelhead," Perin says. "Joe never gave up."

Randolph was even more determined when he had a client in his boat, doing whatever was necessary to catch the most steelhead on the river, even if it meant committing a mortal steelhead sin: nymphing with a Spey rod. Perin says Randolph was one of the first guides to adopt the cheeseburger rig—a Double Bead Peacock Stonefly and Lightning Bug dropper fished beneath a strike indicator—and every time one of his clients cast that meaty monstrosity with a sophisticated Spey rod, it was a virtual middle finger to the purists who believed steelhead should only be caught on the swing with a more traditional wet fly. While Randolph's aggressive tactics pissed off other guides, they paid off. Because on a river where one fish a day is often considered good, Randolph was upset if his boat didn't land a dozen, and when a guide puts up steelhead numbers like that, word spreads fast.

"I've been lucky to fish with guides from New Zealand to Russia, and a lot of places in between," Perin says. "Joe was one of the most popular guides

I've seen anywhere in the world. He had a following of customers like you wouldn't believe."

COACH

Standing in the parking lot outside a grocery store in Sisters, Mark Few noticed a tall guy come out carrying a case of PBR. Few watched as the stranger set the beer into a trailered drift boat, then called out: "Where are you going?"

"Steelhead fishing," Randolph said.

"Steelhead fishing?"

At that, Randolph turned and realized that the guy he'd been talking to was Mark Few—as in Mark Few, men's basketball coach at Gonzaga University, one of the country's elite teams. Randolph was a diehard college hoops fan, and Few had fished his whole life. The two hit it off instantly.

It was early in the steelhead season, and Randolph was going out to scout. They exchanged numbers, and Randolph promised to call once the fish arrived. Later that summer, Few got a phone call. "Coach," Randolph said. He always called him Coach. "They're in." Few met Randolph at Mack's Canyon, and they caught close to 30 steelhead . . . in one day.

"The most unbelievable day of fishing I've ever had," Few says. "It was unreal."

Few respected how Randolph wasn't afraid to try new things to catch more fish. He was impressed by how well Randolph knew the Deschutes. And he loved how positive Randolph always appeared—how his attitude brightened the life around him, including the steelhead. "Joe had great mojo with the fish," Few says.

After that trip, Few never fished the Deschutes with any guide but Randolph.

*****

The Thingamabobber above my cheeseburger rig dunked under the water at Steely Flats, and I tried to set the hook. When I felt nothing, I tried again. Then a fish jumped.

LIFE, DEATH, AND STEELHEAD

Any doubt that I'd come tight to a fish vanished when I heard one of the loudest, most guttural cries in my life: "STEELHEAD ON!" Randolph's shout might've stopped my heart if I weren't already terrified enough of losing my first steelhead. I'd never seen someone come to life like that over a fish—especially a fish someone else caught. I landed and released the wild steelhead, but before I could think about celebrating or resting, Randolph told me to get back to fishing. One steelhead a day wasn't enough.

FLORENCE

In the beginning, Florence was excited for her husband. She could see how much he loved guiding and how good he was at it. He was funny and personable and a patient teacher, and he'd always taken a deep interest in helping people. "Guiding was perfect for him," she says.

After a while, though, Florence began to see that the job wasn't perfect for them. Guiding is one thing when you don't have a family, but she and Randolph had a family—a pretty big one, too. "When you have all these kids, guiding just doesn't provide enough money—and there's no medical coverage, none of those things," Florence says. "That was the beginning of some issues." To make matters worse, the more popular Randolph became on the river, the less time he could spend at home with his family.

JEFF

To go with the athletic talent and raw determination, Perin can point to one other factor that made Randolph, his ace guide, such a great steelhead fisherman—and it might have been the most significant factor of all, certainly the hardest to explain. Randolph was, quite simply, as fishy as they get. His instincts, so in tune with the waters and the fish, were so sharp that the people who know fishing, and knew Randolph—people like Perin—struggle to describe him any other way. "Joe was just fishy." Randolph was fishy everywhere he fished, but nowhere was he fishier than on the Deschutes. He knew every rock, seam, and crevice. He knew where the steelhead held and what they'd bite. He lived for that river.

"Joe felt a connection to life when he was on the Deschutes," Perin says.

"That river had a pulse that somehow beat with the same pulse of Joe's heart."

*****

When we broke for camp at Harris Canyon, I was more than ready to get off the water. My knees hurt from too many slips on the rocks, and my hands and arms ached from too many bad casts. I was tired and cold and just wanted to rest. Randolph let me sit long enough for a swig of Fireball and a few sips of beer before he told me to get back on the river and fish the stretch that ran along camp.

Even though Randolph was only trying to give me more time on the water so I could hopefully catch another steelhead, I resented him for staying back at camp, relaxing and drinking. At least he'd finally let me use the one-handed fly rod that I'd brought along. Compared to the Spey rod, it felt like a feather and was easier on my arm. But I'd gotten used to the bigger stick, and now my casting went to shambles. I was struggling to untangle the tippet when, impulsively, I turned around: There was Randolph, holding a Spey rod for me to use. I don't know how long he'd been watching, but for the rest of the way, until I finished the run, he stayed by my side.

FLORENCE

In summer 2008, Randolph's kids, Hank and Maddi, moved back to California; their mother had regained custody. Once they were gone, the man Florence Belmondo had thought she would grow old with was never the same. "He went into guiding 100 percent," she says, "and let go of everything else."

COACH

A day on the Deschutes is never leisurely—but it was even less so when Coach Few and Randolph fished together. The night before a trip, Few would drive down from Washington. If he made good time, he'd reach the Mack's Canyon launch by 3 a.m. and unfold a cot and sleep until Randolph arrived. By 4:30 a.m. they'd be on the water. Twenty-six miles later, around

10 p.m., they would take out at the mouth of the Columbia River where the Deschutes ends.

For just about every other guide on the Deschutes, the trip from Mack's to the mouth would be spread across at least two days, sometimes three. To float it in one day demanded a guide who was bold and devoted—but also smart. Randolph was that guide, and Few loved him for it. "We had the same mind-set when we fished," Few says. "We tried to have a great time, but we fished hard. Really, really hard."

Competing guides would see Randolph haul ass past them in his drift boat, and must have simultaneously cursed him for getting to the next hole faster and questioned him for skipping so much good water. What those guides might not have understood was that to cover so much water in one day, Randolph had to be hyperselective in the holes he fished. During a day float that long, he had time for maybe six stops—but they'd be the very best six stops, and Randolph would fish them for all they were worth. An angler like Coach Few could pull tight on 10 steelhead in one hole. "If you went with Joe," Few says, "you hooked a lot of fish."

When the mouth of the Columbia River finally appeared, Few would go home—but not Randolph. It was nothing for him to schedule three, four, or five Mack's-to-the-mouth trips in a row. As soon as one ended, he'd immediately drive all the way back upriver that night. If he was lucky, he might get to sleep for a few hours before he had to be on the water again at 4:30 a.m.

ALEX

Randolph saw something in Alex Gonsiewski. Gonsiewski was hired on as a guide at the Fly Fisher's Place in 2009, and Randolph took a quick liking to him. Like Randolph, Gonsiewski wanted to turn over every river rock to see what was under it. Like Randolph, Gonsiewski wanted to float the whole river in a day, trailer the boat, run back to the dock, and do it all over again. Like Randolph, Gonsiewski had made up his mind that fishing would be the most important thing in his life.

When the two had time off that coincided, they'd fill the cooler with beer and PB&Js and hit the Deschutes for days, and on those trips Randolph taught Gonsiewski the river. He showed him how to float Mack's to the mouth in one day. He shared some of his best spots. He helped Gonsiewski become a better guide—and he did that by letting Gonsiewski know how much he believed in him.

"Joe thought I had it," Gonsiewski says. "I think that's part of the reason people liked fishing with him so much. He was good at making people feel really confident about themselves."

FLORENCE

All her husband seemed to care about was fishing, and the only place he seemed at peace was the Deschutes. If he wasn't guiding, he'd disappear— for days, even weeks, at a time. He'd come home for a spell, then leave again. Sometimes he'd call to check in; other times not.

"Fishing was his escape," Florence says. "That way he didn't have to think too much about the fact that he wasn't with his kids. Some people think they can escape by doing something they enjoy. But you can't be doing that 24/7. You have moments where everything else comes back."

They divorced in January 2009.

ALEX

It took him a bit longer, but Gonsiewski saw something in Randolph, too. Spend as much time with a person as Gonsiewski did with his friend and coworker, and it would've been hard to miss. Gonsiewski saw a guide who was burdened and stressed by his high-profile clients who'd gotten too used to catching 10 steelhead a day and now demanded too much of Randolph. He saw a father who, as much as he said he missed his kids, made little effort to get them back or stay in touch; a man who regretted things that had happened in his life off the water, who lived with plenty of heartache. He saw that for as much confidence as Randolph gave others, he had very little of his own.

"Most days, if you looked in his eyes," Gonsiewski says, "there wasn't a lot there."

After breakfast, we floated down to a small island very close to camp. Randolph tied a Cold Medicine—a big, bright streamer with hollowed barrel eyes—on my line and told me to swing it through the current, then take two steps down after each cast until I reached the end of the run.

It was 8:15 a.m. when I was standing in the middle of the pool, and a burst from the river scorched all the way up my fishing line like a lit fuse before it reached the reel and exploded in my right hand. I hardly had a chance to react before I heard, once again, that gorgeous cry.

"STEELHEAD ON!"

BRENDA

She remembers moments when she wasn't the best mom. She remembers her own battles with depression, and she thinks about how they must have impacted her son. She remembers when Joe, after he'd moved out, began to distance himself from her. She remembers how, on the rare occasions she might see her son, he was always warm and cordial, but their past was never far behind.

KAY

Joe moved to Oregon without ever saying goodbye. To this day, Kay still doesn't know why her brother, as an adult, pushed her away. "Maybe it was pride," she says. "Maybe it was something else." She thought that the two of them—as close as they'd once been—could've worked through any problem together. Joe was never willing to try, but she was. She'd call him in Oregon, and sometimes he'd actually pick up. She'd ask how he was holding up, and mention the idea of coming to visit, because it would've been so nice to see him and because she loved the thought of her brother taking her husband and son fishing. Joe never got back to her on that.

*****

My casting had gotten better. I no longer felt like I had to focus on every little motion of every single cast. As the actions came more naturally, my thoughts drifted. I thought about my wife of only a few months and what she was doing

back home. I thought of work and what would be waiting for me. I thought of some-
thing Randolph had said when I asked him why he loved coming to the Deschutes.
   "Because you don't have to think," he'd said.

JEFF

For some guides, the end of the steelhead season each winter meant the chance to do something new until next year's run. "For Joe," Perin says, "it was like the end of the world."

Come winter, Randolph's home was no longer the river but his house, where he was alone and where troubling reminders of his divorce, estranged children, and increasing debt consumed him.

One day in 2011, around Christmas, Perin noticed some of the camping gear the Fly Fisher's Place used for guide trips was missing. And one of the drift boats was gone. Perin called the shuttle driver, who confirmed what he'd feared: Randolph had taken the boat. State police dispatched search crews in a Cessna and jet boat and found Randolph riding the Deschutes, alone in the cold.

This was the second winter in a row that Randolph had given Perin and other friends in Sisters cause for alarm. But unlike his first attempt, this time Randolph had not left a note. When Randolph was back safe in town, Perin asked him point-blank: "You tried to kill yourself last year. Did you go down the river to try and do it again?"

"I went down there to think about doing it," he said.

*****

We hadn't gone very far—a mile at most. It was already past noon, and we still
had plenty of river to go before we reached the mouth. Randolph decided we
should make a big push downriver to Power Line Hole. We'd have to skip some
good water to get there, but he promised it'd be worth it, as long as we were first.
"We could pull 10 fish outta there if no one's messed with it," he said. "Could be
one fish, but it'll at least be one."
   Once we arrived at Power Line Hole, something seemed off. The water was
fast and up to my chest—but not so much faster or deeper than other spots I'd

fished so far. And in those spots, while I might've slipped here and there, I could at least stand still. At Power Line Hole, I could not. It felt like I was skating on the boulders, and because I was positioned near the ledge of a deep dropoff, that wasn't a good feeling. Meanwhile, Randolph was chilling in the anchored boat, smoking and drinking.

"Wade deeper!" he yelled.

I didn't dare move. One wrong step, and I feared that I'd lose my balance and be swept downcurrent in a river that claims a few lives every year. I tried to cast but failed miserably. Whatever comfort or rhythm I'd found earlier had vanished. I was terrified. Not even Randolph's promise of one fish—maybe 10—was enough to keep me on that ledge.

Gingerly, I took one step backward, then another, and another until I was in safe, shallow water. Randolph didn't say a word to me as I trudged back. I could tell he was disappointed. After I climbed into the boat on my own, I looked at the bottom of my boots: The rock-gripping felt soles on both had completely worn off, claimed by the Deschutes.

JEFF

In 2012, Randolph moved from Sisters to Maupin—a decision Perin believes Randolph made to get away from the support group of friends that had come together to keep an eye on him. "I think he finally decided he didn't want us on top of him," Perin says. "The best way to do that was to move a couple hours away." Whatever the reason, Randolph's troubles—the loved ones he missed, money he owed—followed him.

That summer, in mid July, he was scheduled to guide three trips in three days for the Fly Fisher's Place. After the first trip, those first-time clients—not knowing any better—tipped Randolph just $25, which he drained into his gas tank. When the second trip ended, the clients told Randolph they'd put his tip on their credit-card bill with the shop instead of giving him cash. Randolph raged. As he sped home that night, he left furious voicemails for Perin, saying that he had no money and nothing to eat. He accused Perin of holding back tips. The day of the third trip, Randolph stood up his clients.

Perin scrambled to find the clients a replacement guide. Then, left with no other choice, he fired Randolph, the greatest steelhead guide he'd ever known.

ALEX

Gonsiewski also left the Fly Fisher's Place in 2012—but on good terms. He went to another outfitter where he could get more clients, earn more money, and keep making a name for himself as one of the best young guides on the Deschutes. He and Randolph remained close friends.

Gonsiewski and Randolph used to kick around the idea of starting their own outfitter, but as exciting as the prospect was, Gonsiewski never took it too seriously because he knew Randolph too well. "Joe was good on the river, but the other stuff that comes with having an outfit—the bookkeeping, running a website—was not Joe's forte," Gonsiewski says. "He didn't have the drive or ability to get better at those things. He knew that, and I think it bothered him."

After he was fired, Randolph began guiding illegally on the Deschutes, taking clients on the water without insurance or a permit. Breaking the law must've seemed easier than running a business.

JEFF

Shortly after their falling out, Perin learned that Randolph had been stealing clients. Randolph was contacting former anglers of his, convincing them to cancel trips with the Fly Fisher's Place so he could guide them instead. Perin fumed. He'd lost thousands of dollars and couldn't afford to let Randolph continue. A few other Oregon outfitters who learned of Randolph's actions took Perin's side. Together they alerted state police of Randolph's renegade outfit. Randolph was ticketed and ordered to appear in court, where his life as a steelhead guide would've likely been suspended, if not ended.

Randolph never spoke to Perin again.

For years, Randolph had distanced himself from people who for one reason or another he wanted out of his life. Now, through acts all his own, the Deschutes River and guiding—the only things in his life he seemed determined to keep as close as possible—had been taken away from him.

LIFE, DEATH, AND STEELHEAD

*I asked Randolph if my busted wading boots would limit where we could fish.
"Yeah," he said. For a time after that, I didn't hear a word from him.*

ALEX

One rare day off between guide trips last November, Gonsiewski heard that
Randolph was missing. He knew Randolph had gone on floats before and
just not told anyone, and he hoped that was the case this time. But knowing
Randolph as well as he did, Gonsiewski worried.

Gonsiewski left his friend a couple of voice messages, asking where he
was. He waited as long as he could, hoping to hear back, before he had to
leave for another multiday trip on the Deschutes.

*****

*We had to skip Triangle Hole because it was too deep and slick for me. At the next
hole, Randolph literally had to hold my hand as we walked across the boulders. I
was humiliated. We tried a few spots that were shallow enough for me to wade,
but I could tell that Randolph's heart was not in it. At this point, we were just
killing time.*

ALEX

The day Gonsiewski got off the river from his trip, he checked his phone to
see if Randolph had called. Instead, he found a message from his old boss,
Jeff Perin.

Police had found Randolph dead inside his car, parked near a patch of
woods outside of town with a garden hose snaking from the tailpipe into
his vehicle.

*****

*I hated the thought that I'd disappointed Randolph, after he'd worked so hard
to put me on fish. He could've used my wardrobe malfunction as an excuse to
end the trip early—and, honestly, I wouldn't have argued. I was too tired and*

defeated. I was ready to give up on steelhead. But Randolph wasn't ready, because there was still river to fish.

He never gave up on me and he never put me down. Instead, he did what only the best guide would've done: He found safer water, stuck the rod in my hand, and told me to keep fishing. And an hour later, after the Spey rod buckled under the strength of my third wild steelhead, Randolph was there to help me release it back into the Deschutes, alive and strong.

JEFF

He misses those early days—before Randolph's rise to steelhead fame, before they worked together—when Randolph would come into the Fly Fisher's Place and hang out and laugh. He misses the days when they were just friends.

BRENDA

She remembers her son's heart, his sweet heart. She remembers him as loving and vulnerable. She remembers, and misses most, those big hugs.

ALEX

The first time Gonsiewski floated Mack's to the mouth again was hard. Not seeing Randolph at the bar is hard. Days off, when Gonsiewski likes to fish, are real hard. "He was my fishing buddy," Gonsiewski says. "I was always good at just having one fishing buddy because you don't need more than one."

KAY

She wants her nephew and niece to know she'll do whatever she can for them. She wants them to know how much their father really did love them.

She'd want her brother to know his son and daughter are doing O.K. "They're great kids," Kay says. "For all they've been through, they're great kids."

LIFE, DEATH, AND STEELHEAD

COACH

Mark Few isn't sure what this fishing season will be like. He loves the Deschutes too much to stay away. And when he does return, he'll bring with him all he learned from Randolph—the nymph rigs, the casting lessons, the knowledge of the river. And he'll always bring that belief.

"Coach," Randolph used to tell him, "it's great to fish with you because you just know you're gonna catch a fish. You've got that belief."

FLORENCE

It's happened a few times since last November: She'll be in town and notice a tall guy wearing the same style of hat and board shorts that he used to wear, and instantly in her mind—before she has a chance to remind herself that he couldn't be, that he cannot be—she sees him.

*****

He plowed downstream, racing the surviving daylight, until we reached Grasshopper Hole. I started swinging a Cold Medicine through the run without any instruction from Randolph until he called out and pointed to a boulder sticking halfway out of the water a hundred yards downstream. "As soon as the end of your line touches that rock—" he yelled, then mimed calling it quits.

I nodded, but as I worked my way downriver something changed. The closer I came to the boulder, the farther away I wanted it to be. A few hours earlier, I would've given anything to reel up and abandon this river. But now I wanted to stay. Because here, at our last stop, everything that Randolph taught me had taken hold. My rod traveled the same orbit on every cast. My line glided through the guides. My fly unrolled and dropped gently in the current. And so I went from taking two steps after each cast, to one step. Then from one step to a half step. I believed my steelhead was out there, on whatever rock I was casting to, and I was determined to catch it. So I kept casting and casting and casting—more and more hopeful after each that my line would pull tight—until finally, after my fly was swinging far past the boulder, I accepted the last cast and gave up.

I walked back to the boat where Randolph was waiting at the bow, smiling.

He didn't say so, but he must've noticed that I'd fished farther than I was told. Maybe he didn't say anything because he understood why I couldn't stop. Maybe he let me keep going because he didn't want to leave the Deschutes either.

"Good job," he said.

"Thanks."

He eased the drift boat into the blackening river. The sun had fallen, and the river was quiet and calm until the current carried us to Rattlesnake Rapids, one last test before the mouth. The white-capped water pulsed beneath us. Chop slapped the hull as the boat began to bob and gain speed. He pulled back on the oars, and just as he had so many times in his life—with new clients and old friends, with the people he loved and the ones he kept in his heart—Joe Randolph rode the Deschutes to the end.

VERTICAL TROUT

BOB BUTZ

Two thousand feet down in Colorado's Black Canyon, the Gunnison River is as close to "unrunnable" as a river can get. This is Class V and VI water—a 20-mile-stretch of angry, killer, boulder-strewn white water—a short drive northwest of Montrose. But from the top of the North Rim, peering down between those sheer granite walls pressing in as smooth as tombstones, the river far below looks like a tiny emerald hair. Word is that the trout swimming there, rainbows and browns, are bigger than the blade of a canoe paddle. The trouble is how to reach them.

Given the altitude and the sheerness of the walls, I wondered if a base jump might not be a more practical means of descent. Our plan included packs, sleeping bags, and tents. Harnesses. Helmets. Ropes. And fly rods.

It's called "cast and climb," and it's a technique finding favor in such places as Bar Habor, Maine, and the other Black Canyon in Yellowstone Park. The idea is insane, but simple: Big fish survive best where people do not, and so you look for a piece of water that is so inaccessible that it might as well be on the other side of the world.

There were four of us making the climb down into "The Black," as it's known in Colorado—a Michigander (myself), and three Montanans: Dave

Long, a former molecular biologist turned photographer; Lee Hewey, a contractor; and Tony Demin, another photographer. It was the mother of all descents—but what lay at the bottom was worth it.

It was Tony who found the trail, if you can call it that: more like a sheep path pitching down, a few degrees shy of vertical, through a slipping and sliding chute of loose talus toward the canyon floor. Park rangers (the Black Canyon is the heart of Colorado's Gunnison National Park) describe this descent as a "controlled fall." Local rock climbers refer to it as the S.O.B. Draw. Whatever you call it, a little over half an hour into the climb, I was sweating hard and breathing through my mouth, my knees ready to buckle.

We tacked back and forth over the ankle-twisting talus, scrambling over boulders and rubble, losing the trail and then finding it again, while the heat shimmered off the rust-colored walls of the canyon. We kept our eyes on the rocks underfoot, matching step for step with the man in front as an eagle soared overhead and swallows darted from their nests in the rock.

There are two constant dangers here: One is falling, and the other is poison ivy, which Steve Lyons described in his Black Canyon guidebook as "gargantuan, lush and potent, shiny-green-leaved bushes that crowd and hover over the trail."

The river came into view, roaring, and spitting white between cabin-size boulders. It took us nearly three hours to make it to the bottom, where the canyon floor, strewn with millions of years' worth of falling rock, offered not one square foot of level ground. Everywhere were giant ramps of talus, piles of stone, and immense, precariously balanced boulders.

Near the base of the trail we descended, the Gunnison is almost completely blocked off by a colossal wall of rubble, silo-shaped granite blocks with—seemingly—no handholds and no way to climb over them. But on the other side was a pool that, from 2,000 feet up, had suggested prime fishing—and in fact may never have been fished before.

Our plan was to make camp and try to climb the wall the following morning. So we followed the current downstream along an ankle-turning footpath, and after a mile found one of the few places that you can pitch a tent in the canyon. It was a grassy spot about the size of a putting green, at the base of a talus slope. We pitched the tents and ate lunch. Tony headed off with his camera and tripod. Dave went in search of a way over the wall for the next day with Hewey along to belay him, and I sat at the river's edge, kneading my aching thighs.

But I had come to fish. So I tried the big pool that our campsite overlooked, a place I came to call Disappointment Hole. Boiling rapids, the water fizzing like seltzer, marked its head and foot. Here the Gunnison runs a frigid 45 degrees and the current is so swift you don't want to wade in above your knees. Heeding the advice of park rangers, I didn't want to wade in at all. I hopped from rock to rock along the river's edge, frustrated by trout just out of reach and cracking at every midge and mayfly in the pool except the imitations tied to my leader.

Black caddis, bluewing olive, an Adams—they wanted none of it. I toiled away most of the afternoon without a bite. Finally, I tried casting nymphs—a prince, and a pheasant tail on a dropper—to a seam where the river split between two chalky stones, and was fast connected to a fish.

It was a good-size rainbow that swam a few wild circles in the hole, and I almost had it in hand when something exploded in the river like a depth charge. Then another—a rock the size of a football, followed by a handful of smaller stones. I looked up to the crack of sky above me and saw only the canyon walls glowing pink and rusty in the sun.

My rainbow had broken off, and finding it difficult to fish with one eye on the water and the other searching the sky for rocks that could break my skull, I worked my way back to camp, troutless.

The ascent over the rubble dam was more of a crawl than a climb. We couldn't get all the way over it, so after scraping and cussing our way 20 feet up onto a narrow ledge, we literally crawled through it. We inched through crevasses and belly-crawled through fissures and wormholes between the stones. Down a ramp of granite, bare of holds, we worked to another ledge, reaching the bottom of the gorge at last—and another wall.

It was shady and cool and damp. Although we could hear the river ripping under us and the rumble of loose stones rolling with the current vibrating beneath our heels, we could see no water. Dave pointed to a dark crack in the wall.

"We're going through there next."

When I did see water again it was inside that mass of huge stones—a narrow chute of gushing white froth that we had to half straddle, half hop over. We crawled over damp driftwood, the road of the river echoing off the walls, and then finally there was a light and a hole overhead through which we emerged one by one like marmots, happy in the sun.

The first thing I saw was a trout in the green water, sucking midges from the top—big trout, a dozen or so, their shadow forms finning in the current. The rainbows were hefty, slab-sided, mustard-colored fish with a wide raspberry stripe down their sides. The most striking thing about them was their eyes—bulbous, round goldfish eyes, formed by a life passed in this canyon where the direct sun only shines a couple of hours a day.

While the rainbows were easily as long as my hand and forearm, the browns were smaller but decidedly better fighters. We pulled them by the dozens from swirling holes and eddies no bigger than the hood of a pickup. Anywhere there was slack water the fish were stacked like cordwood, and we caught them as you would expect to in a place that few fishermen have even seen, let alone wet a line in.

I've always been of a mind that water is a little sweeter when you mix it with sweat. Although the trout were what brought us here, they would have to take a backseat to the challenge of getting in, the climb through the dam, the next day's long, hard ascent out of the canyon—and, of course, the chance of getting killed in the process. All to find a quiet place on the water, which leads the flyfishing obsessive in me to wonder: *Has it really come to this?*

QUEST

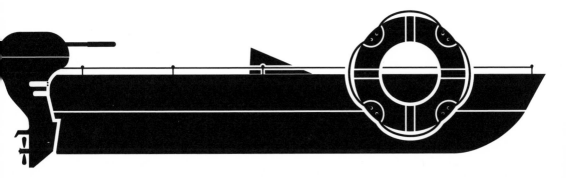

THE DESCENT

T. EDWARD NICKENS

The idea that there are two Alaskas came to me in a cold wave as my canoe was swept into the toppled trees and I was thrown overboard. I caught a glimpse of my pal, Scott Wood, sprinting toward me across a gravel bar, knowing that this was what we had feared the most. Wood disappeared into the brush, running for my life, and then the river sucked me under and I did not see anything else for what seemed like a very long time.

Every angler dreams of Alaska. My dream was of untouched waters, uncountable salmon and trout, and an unguided route through mountains and tundra. But day after day of portages and hairy paddling had suggested that mine was a trip to the other Alaska, a place that suffers no prettied-up pretense. The other Alaska is not in brochures. It is rarely in dreams. The other Alaska will kill you.

We'd had plenty of postcard moments, for sure: king salmon jetting rooster tails over gravel bars. Tundra hills pocked with snow. Monster rainbows and sockeye salmon heaving for oxygen as we held their sagging bellies. But day after day the four of us had paddled through the other Alaska, scared to death, except when the fishing was good enough to make us forget the fear.

Now the world turned black and cold as the Kipchuk River covered me, my head underwater, my arm clamped around a submerged tree, my body pulled horizontal in the hurtling current. Lose my grip and the river would sweep me into a morass of more downed trees, so I held on even tighter as water filled my waders. The river felt like a living thing, attempting to swallow me, inch by inch, and all I could do was hold my breath and hang on.

But I am getting ahead of the story.

Give me a canoe, paddle, portage pack, and time, and I can make it down almost any river. For years I've considered this a given, and remote rivers have been my express route to fish that have never seen a fly.

It may be that no one had attempted what we set out to do last July: Complete a 10-day unguided canoe descent of southwestern Alaska's Kipchuk and Aniak Rivers. These are isolated headwaters in the extreme: To get bodies and gear on the ground required five flights in two-person Piper Cub and Super Cub bush planes. Our largest duffels carried 17-foot PakBoats—folding canoes on aluminum frames—which I figured to be our masterstroke. This was part of the dream too: Instead of a ponderous raft, I'd paddle a sleek canoe, catching eddies and exploring side channels. Or so I'd planned.

There were four in the party: myself, photographer Colby Lysne, my friend Edwin Aguilar, and Scott Wood, who more times than not can be found in the other end of whatever canoe I inhabit. Dropping through tundra, we'd first negotiate the Kipchuk through a 1,000-foot-deep canyon. Then we'd slip into the Kuskokwim lowlands, where the river carves channels through square-mile gravel bars and unravels in braids until it flows into the larger Aniak. Some of the most remote country left in Alaska, it is the second-largest watershed in the state, with just a handful of native settlements. We timed our launch for a shot at four of the five Alaska salmon species—kings, pinks, sockeyes, and chums—with a wild-card chance for coho and the Alaska Grand Slam of salmon. We'd been counting our fish for months.

Truth be told, though, no one really knew what to expect on the Kipchuk. According to our bush pilot, Rob Kinkade, less than a handful of hunting parties raft the upper river each year. He'd heard of no one who'd fished above the canyon, ever. As for the paddling conditions—well, he said, it all looked workable from the windshield of a Super Cub.

But we weren't paddling a plane.

The first test came fast, just after put-in. A fallen spruce blocked the channel, with barely enough room to shoulder past. The obstacle looked easy enough to handle, but the water was swift and heavy, and the laden boats were slower to react than we'd imagined. Wood and Aguilar fought to cross a racing tongue of current and were carried straight for the spruce. Watching from upstream, I could hear Wood barking over the rush of water—"Draw right! Right! Harder! Harder!"—as the canoe slipped closer to the tree. They cleared by inches. Wood glanced at us, knowing what we were in for.

"So," Lysne said, his eyes on the water. "That didn't look so good."

Already we were feeling our handicap. With a flyover scouting report of no whitewater, Wood and I had dialed back the level of paddling experience we expected from our partners. Lysne and Aguilar had plenty of remote camps in the bag, but they'd never been whitewater cowboys. Cocksure with a canoe paddle, I figured—as did Wood—that we could handle whatever came up from the stern. What came up was a paddler's worst nightmare: miles of strainers.

Where sharp turns occur, the current undercuts the channel's outside bank. As the bank collapses, trees fall, wedging against the shore. Water gets through, but a canoe carried into a strainer has little chance of remaining upright—and a body slammed into the underwater structure has little chance of escape.

Rattled, Lysne and I slipped into the fast water and tried to crab the boat sideways with short draw strokes. A big-handed North Dakota hockey player, Lysne tackles obstacles with a brawler's bravado—a frame of mind that would pay off later. I started to yell as we neared the strainer, and for a second I caught Wood's concerned look, knowing that in the next moment, the boat would tangle sideways in the spruce and our fishing trip would turn into a rescue operation.

I paddled the strongest half-dozen strokes of my life as the spruce boughs raked across Lysne's shoulders and caught me in the chest. We pulled away, inch by inch. My heart was pounding. We sidled up to the other PakBoat.

THE DESCENT

"We cannot capsize," Wood said, his face intense. "You know that. We simply cannot capsize."

That night we calmed our nerves with Scotch and pan-fried Arctic grayling, whose bodies had spilled out whole mice when we cleaned them a few hundred feet from our campsite. Wine-red shapes coursed up the pool—king salmon that ignored our flies. But it was early. With each paddle stroke, the fishing should only get better, the paddling easier. I crawled into the tent feeling like a dog clipped by a car. Tomorrow, we figured, it would all come together.

But tomorrow was the day the canyon closed in.

This stretch of the river was filled with more dread and sweat than we'd bargained for—and far less fishing. Every turn in the Kipchuk was a blind bend. Every bend was lined with downed trees. And each time the river narrowed, a chute of blistering midstream flow formed a hard wall of current that threatened to flip the boats.

We were also running a different kind of uncharted waters. Though Wood and I have been to spots where getting through the country proved difficult and dangerous, never had we experienced day after day of serious peril. We wanted the Alaskan wilds, and we didn't mind pain and sweat for a payoff of unknown country. A taste of fear was part of the price. But on the Kipchuk, we were gagging on terror.

"There was a time," Wood said, standing on the bank three days into the canyon, "when I liked being scared in the woods. It made it all seem so . . . real." His voice trailed off, and his gaze followed downriver. I knew where his thoughts were taking him. Mine were already there. Home. Wife. Children. "I don't like being scared anymore," he said.

Lysne and I pushed the canoe into the river without saying a word. I could only imagine what he was thinking. Lysne never complained, never pointed out that he'd signed on to photograph a fishing trip, not an adrenaline rush down a rain-swollen river. I didn't voice the thoughts coursing through my own head. The cheerful scouting report notwithstanding, I'd had no business putting inexperienced paddlers in such remote, unknown water. My arrogance was shameful, and the dangers were accruing. Humping gear and dragging boats through 20-foot-tall thickets, where a feeding bear would be invisible at 10 feet, was a necessity. But that's the seduction of wilderness travel. Each time you come back, you think you can handle more. Until you can't.

Downstream, the river disintegrated. On the banks, water boiled through 10-foot-tall walls of downed timber as the Kipchuk careened around hairpin turns. Time and time again we roped the canoes around the roughest water, but too often the only choice was to carry everything. To portage the hairpins, we bushwhacked through thickets, taking turns as point man with the shotgun and bear spray. We hacked trails through streamside saplings. We fished in spurts—10 minutes here, 15 there. It took all we had just to keep going.

One night I crouched beside the campfire, nursing blisters and a bruised ego. My back felt like rusted wire. Lysne limped in pain, his toes swollen and oozing pus. I was tired of portaging, tired of paddling all day with little time for fishing, tired of fear. I watched Lysne take a swig of Costa Rican guaro.

"I have to be honest with you," he muttered. "I've had some dark times the last few days. Been f---ing scared and I'm not afraid to say it."

The night before, he said, he'd dreamed that we were paddling through a swamp, but it was inside somebody's garage, and a fluorescent alligator attacked the canoe.

"Weird, huh? I wonder where that came from."

The next morning I dragged myself out of the tent with a mission. Somewhere, downriver, the other Alaska waited.

"Today we paddle like madmen," I suggested.

"Yeah," Aguilar groused. "We need to quit being such slackers."

A few miles downstream we lined a run and dragged the canoes to the head of a deep pool the color of smoke and emeralds. A half dozen large fish held near the upstream ledge. I slid a rod out of the canoe. The first cast landed a pink salmon. My second brought in a chum. I hooted as Aguilar fumed and glanced at his watch.

"Ten minutes!" I pleaded. "I promise, just 10 minutes!"

He huffed and grabbed a rod. Fishing chaos broke out. Wood, Lysne, and I worked a triple hookup on salmon, our lines crossing. We fought sockeyes, kings, and wolf-fanged chum salmon. We landed 3-pound grayling and a solid 26-inch rainbow. One fish ran up the rapids at the head of the pool, leaping like a silver kite. Another was so close that it splashed me.

For the first time I felt the pieces coming together. The pull of strong fish was a poultice for ragged nerves and sore shoulders.

Eleven salmon steaks, slathered in chipotle sauce, sizzled over the fire that night.

"We deserved today," Aguilar said, lying back on a bed of rocks.

"Fishing is fun," added Wood. "We should try to do more of it."

Late the next afternoon, we beached the boats to fish another salmon-choked pool, and in less than a minute we were shoulder to shoulder, working a quadruple hookup. Lysne cackled as my king ran under his bent rod.

It was a fine place to camp and a good time to call it quits, but I'm not fond of camping above a hairy rapid. Just below the pool, a pair of fallen spruce trees leaned over the main channel, then the river bent hard, the bank combed with strainers.

"Let's get this over with," I muttered. "We can celebrate when there's clear sailing ahead."

"Sure," Wood replied. "But we were first on the last horrible, terrible, death-for-certain river bend. You're up."

The next half minute, Wood would later say, seemed to last an hour. Entering the river, Lysne and I lined up with the route we'd hashed out. Once the laden canoe sliced into the main current tongue, however, it was propelled downstream with terrifying speed. Draw strokes didn't budge us. Pry strokes and stern rudders proved useless. I lost my hat as we rocketed under the timber. The craft arrowed into a wall of downed trees and suddenly we were tangled in branches, broadside to the current, water boiling against the hull.

"Don't lean upstream!" I screamed. Lysne didn't, but in the next instant the river swarmed over the gunwales anyway. The boat flipped, violently, and disappeared from view.

The current sucked me under. I caught a submerged tree trunk square in the chest, a blow buffered by my PFD, and I clamped an arm around the slick trunk.

I can't say how long I hung there. Twenty seconds, perhaps? Forty?

For long moments I knew I wouldn't make it. With my free arm, I pulled myself along the sunken trunk as the current whipped me back and forth. But the trunk grew larger and larger. It slipped from the grip of my right armpit, and then I held fast to a single branch, groping for the next with my other hand. I don't remember holding my breath. I don't remember the frigid water. I just remember that the thing that was swallowing me had its grip on my shins, then my knees, and then my thighs. For an odd few moments I heard a metallic ringing in my ears. A vivid scene played across my brain: It was the telephone in my kitchen at home, and it was ringing, and Julie was walking through the house looking for the phone, and I suddenly knew that if she answered the call—was the phone on the coffee table? did the kids have it in the playroom?—that the voice on the other end of the line would be apologetic and sorrowful. Then the toe of my boot dragged on something hard, and I stood up, and I could breathe.

Wood crashed through the brush, wild-eyed, as I crawled up the bank, heaving water. I waved him downstream, then clambered to my feet and started running. Somewhere below was Lysne.

The big-handed hockey player had gone overboard farther midstream than I had and vanished beyond the strainers. Stumbling through brush, I heard Wood give a cry, and my heart sank. I burst into sunlight. Wood was facedown on a mud bar, where he'd catapulted after tripping on a root. Aguilar battered his way out of a nearby thicket. A few feet away, Lysne stood chest-deep in the river, with stunned eyes and mouth open. In his hand he gripped the bow line to the canoe, half sunk and turned on its side, the gear bags still secured by rope.

Our ragged little foursome huddled by the river, dumbstruck by the turn of events. For a long time we shook our heads and tried not to meet one another's gazes.

Wood finally looked at Lysne. "I can't believe you saved the boat."

"It was weird," Lysne said, his voice rising. "I popped out of the water and saw another strainer coming for me, and I just got pissed off. I was yelling to myself: I ain't gonna drown! I ain't gonna drown! I went crazy, punching and kicking my way through the trees. Then boom: I saw the rope, grabbed it, and started swimming."

I'd lost a shotgun, two fly rods and reels, and a bag of gear, but everything else that went into the river came out.

Aguilar sidled over, quietly. "You okay? I mean, in your head?"

Only then did I feel the river's grip loosen from my legs. I began to shiver, and no one said a word.

"Salmon. Salmon. Salmon-salmon-salmon." I was counting the kings passing under the boat. Sunlight streamed into the water, lighting up 15-, 20-, and 30-pound chinooks. Downstream, the Kuskokwim lowlands flattened out—no more canyon walls, no more bluffs: slow water and flat country and easy going.

In the bow, Lysne watched the fish and shook his head. "I just spent a week on the Russian River, shoulder-to-shoulder combat fishing," he said. "I can't believe nobody's here. And nobody's been here. And nobody's coming here. Amazing."

I settled into a cadence of easy paddling, the sort that lets the mind drift free. So far, the price of admission to a place where nobody goes had come close to a body bag. I wondered how much longer I'd be willing to shell out for the solitude. Back home were two kids and a wife and a life I've been lucky to piece together. With each year I have more to lose. I'm not ready for an RV and a picnic table, but I couldn't help but wonder if it was time to dial the gonzo back. I didn't know. I won't know, until I hear of the next uncharted river, the next place to catch fish in empty country, and ask myself: What now?

Salmon. Salmon. Salmon-salmon-salmon.

Late in the afternoon we slipped into a deep pool unremarkable but for the 50 kings, pinks, and chums queued up, snout to tail. For 15 minutes they ignored egg-sucking leeches, pink buggers, Clousers, mouse flies, saltwater copperheads, and even a green spoon fly, the go-to choice for hawg bass back home. Downstream, salmon darted across a gravel bar. We could see them coming from 100 yards away.

Wood reeled in and stomped off. He is not one to be snubbed by visible fish. "I'm gonna think outside the koi pond," he said, following grizzly tracks up the sandbar. Ten minutes later we heard a whoop from inside shaking willows. The tip of a fly rod protruded from the thicket, arcing into the water. "Bring your cane poles, boys," Wood hollered.

Worming his way through the brush, Wood had flipped a fly into the gravy train of salmon. It didn't work right away. But ultimately, a pig king had sauntered over to slurp it. No casting, no stripping was required—you just had to keep the fly away from the tykes and hold on. Some of the fish were enormous. Dangling my rod over the salmon, I tried five drifts, 10, no takers, 15 drifts with the pink leech jigged fractions of an inch from the mouths of fish. They stared, looking, looking, l-o-o-o-king, until one sucked it down.

Cackling and howling, the four of us caught king after king, taking turns in the hole. No one cared that this was artless fishing. Dumbed-down salmon whacking was what we needed.

A half hour later, Lysne hooked a brute of a king. The 30-pound chinook never showed until Lysne fought it into the shallows. I went in up to my armpits to land it. My hands barely reached around the base of the tail. Lifting the fish was like pulling a log out of the water. When I handed it to Lysne, he groaned. "We've got to camp right here," he said and grinned. "I don't think I can lift a paddle after this."

Behind him, chum salmon leapt in the air, and kings sent more rooster tails skyward, their backs out of the water. We flopped on the sandbar and fired up a stove. Mist turned into rain as we scrounged the food bag, poured out the juice from a can of smoked mussels, and sautéed jerk-seasoned sockeye in the makeshift frying oil.

Not 3 feet away, a single chum salmon labored upstream. This one was far past spawning. The sight struck me silent: The fish was rotting, its flanks pale and leprous, the spines of its dorsal and tail fins sticking out above the flesh like the shattered masts of a toy sailboat.

The next three days brought the Alaska of my dreams. Now the fish came in schools so large that they appeared as burgundy slicks moving upcurrent. There was nothing easy about coaxing them to a fly, and nothing easy about bringing them to hand. We killed one fish a day, enough to eat like kings. One afternoon I was lying back on rocks near grizzly and wolf tracks so fresh that the prints had not yet dried. "This is what I thought it'd be like every day," Aguilar said. "But now, just one day of it feels so-o-o-o good."

We'd had moments of fish chaos—multiple hookups, the Cane Pole Hole, outrageous rainbow trout. But fishing remote Alaska isn't about the numbers, or the variety of species. It's about the way the fish are seasoned with fear, sweat, miscues, and the mishaps that are the hallmark of an authentic trip in authentic wild country.

On the night before our scheduled pickup, we camped at the juncture of the Aniak and a long, sweeping channel. After setting up the tents, Lysne cooled his heels. His toes were swollen and chinook-red from day after day of hard walking in waders.

"I can't even think about wading right now," he said. "I'm just gonna lie here and fish in my mind."

Wood, Aguilar, and I divvied up the water: They headed off to hunt rainbows down the side channel, while I fished a wide pool on the river.

Since I'd lost my rods and reels when our boat flipped, I fished a cobbled-together outfit of an 8-weight rod with a 9-weight line. It was a little light but heavy enough for the fish we'd landed over the last few days. In an hour of nothing, I made 50 casts to an endless stream of oblong shapes. Then suddenly my hot-pink fly disappeared. Immediately I knew: This was my biggest king, by far. The salmon leapt, drenching my waders, then ripped off line and tore across the current.

The rod bent into the cork, thrumming with the fish's power. I'd have a hard time landing this one solo, so I yelled for help, but everyone was long gone.

So I stood there, alone and undergunned, and drank it all in. It no longer mattered if this was my first or 15th or 30th king salmon. What mattered was that wild Alaska flowed around my feet and pulled at the rod, and I could smell it in the sweet scent of pure water and spruce and in the putrid tang of the dying salmon. I felt it against my legs, an unyielding wildness. Part of what I felt was fear, part of it was respect, and part of it was gratitude that there yet remained places so wild that I wasn't sure I ever wished to return.

Then the king surfaced 5 feet away and glimpsed the source of his trouble. At once the far side of the river was where the salmon wanted to be, and for a long time there was little I could do but hang on.

FIFTY DAYS ON THE WATER

JIM HARRISON

Last May I was at my wit's end, which I admit is never all that far away. Every reader of *Field & Stream* knows that life can be a ceaselessly unpleasant squabble with reality, and that's why you escape to the field to hunt, or to the stream to fish. In my case I had recently experienced two years of wrangling with lawyers, real estate agents, and courts over three properties involved in our move from northern Michigan to Montana. The buyer on the farm we were selling had put 36 contingencies on the sale and had deftly noticed that one survey was 40 feet off. Meanwhile, we had put 52 contingencies on the farm we were buying; plus, the river property where we eventually hoped to build had been virtually condemned as a "floodway."

The move itself wasn't uprooting because I had fished every late summer in Montana, missing only one year since 1968. I am old and vaguely smart enough to know there was nothing particularly novel in my confused situation. Our wounds tend to be shared though our cures can be unique.

One cold and blustery May morning after taking my dog Rose for a walk on a plateau above Livingston, Montana, I came to a grand conclusion. The dog had spent an hour chasing two curlews which led her this way and that until she collapsed. There is a Newtonian principle in bird dog behavior that they run away from you much faster than they return to you so I watched Rose at an ambling distance, then chased her down and loaded her exhausted body into the truck, at which moment I realized that I would never have a nifty, well-ordered life of financial security. The odds against it were as bad as Rose catching a curlew. Down a long hill I could see the serpentine Yellowstone River. I realized that the only possible equilibrium I could offer to my life was to book my friend and guide Danny Lahren for 50 days beginning the next day because the May caddis hatch was rumored to be on the verge of happening.

I've fished with Danny Lahren for the last 15 years, partly from fear of drowning. During my first season on the Yellowstone in 1968 I was still an aggressive wader and went under three times. In the ensuing years I went under a few more times so that when I finally made some of what is called "real" money I started booking Danny and fished from the kind of MacKenzie boat I had wistfully watched passing for years. I realize this is not accessible to everyone but any angler that comes West should save up for a few days with a guide for the very pragmatic reason of seeing how to handle the water. You learn the hot areas you may wish to fish later if you can gain access, not always an easy matter. Most fishermen secretly think they are experts but why not take advantage of an actual expert?

Eastern fishermen can't immediately understand the volume of water they're dealing with on huge western rivers like the Yellowstone or the Upper Missouri. The most valuable tactic you can bring along is the ability to cast well because nearly all other conditions make the skills you learned back East irrelevant. For instance Livingston, Montana, is said to be the second windiest area in the United States. I had several gorgeous days of fishing this year when the wind was gusting from 30 to 50 knots, which blew many terrestrials into the water. These are difficult casting conditions, a profound euphemism, but then you don't want to miss a day of fishing because you can't make the throw. The best thing you can do is a lot of lawn practicing on the windiest days possible. I always carry a couple of light rods (No. 5 Orvis Trident and a T-3) but also a No. 7 Sage overloaded with an 8 line, which can handle the wind if you pause between extreme gusts. One day on the Upper Missouri I could spot the dimples of rising trout in between whitecaps on the broad river. When you reached the rise between the foaming waves the trout would invariably strike. They knew the fly had to be natural because no fisherman would be dumb enough to be out in a gale.

I suspect that at some point nearly every angler becomes sunk within the mystery of water. There is a primitive but totally justified awe. Often when I look at a river I feel a somewhat goofy swelling in my heart. For me? What luck. The idea that fish spend their entire lives in this moving water comes to mind. As a boy of five years on my first trout fishing expedition to the Pine River in Michigan I became obsessed by the idea that truly enormous brown trout lived in the impenetrably dark and deep holes in the river's bends. Later, in my mid-20s, I saw a 23-pound male brown in a trap during a fish count in the Manistee River. A few years ago Chester Marion caught two brown trout in the 12-pound range on the Yellowstone, but then I should remind myself that Chester is a consummate angler and has been fishing this river obsessively for 50 years. I have the same chance of equaling his performance as a mule does winning the Kentucky Derby.

Still, one must try. The May caddis hatch was upon us and the first two days brought nasty weather, with the second day having the additional problem of too many insects. Caddis are wonderful except when clouds are coming up your nose and the trout are only hitting the underwater emergers. I was literally choking on caddis but luckily had a fine bottle of French wine in the boat and was able to flush them. The third day was a bonanza. We caught 17 along the current line of a pool we'd always thought of as insignificant, the kind of water Danny refers to as a "carp pool." This had happened to us before when the temperature had suddenly dropped from 80 to the mid-30s with sleet and snow, and the hen browns had become hyperphagic, literally wild for food against the coming winter, and we caught 30 on a stretch of river we'd always thought of as "dead." There is a sudden urge to jump over in scuba gear despite the many drownings the newspapers report. It would be far safer to ask the local ospreys.

In June we spent a total of six days in three separate trips on the Big Hole south of Butte. The Yellowstone in June was roiling and turgid with snowmelt and carrying enough water to give anyone pause. The Big Hole is relatively discreet and charming but possibly overfished by those in a rush to get there before the ranchers draw off an unhealthy amount of water for irrigation by midsummer. I also strenuously avoid the armada of fishermen drawn by the June salmonfly hatch. A trick is to start earlier than other anglers or a couple hours later. I offer myself the luxury of avoiding a full day of fishing that visiting anglers naturally demand from their guides. I burned out on saltwater flyfishing in the Florida Keys by fishing every day all day for as much as 30 days in a row and now find that four to six hours constitutes a perfect fishing day.

Certain stretches of the Big Hole possess a haunting beauty that constitute what I think of as the prettiest trout stream in America and occasionally the most irritating. You can go through a dozen fly changes and draw a two-hour blank. Curiously it doesn't take a visible hatch to get things started. On a float that began with a considerable spell of disappointment, the fish suddenly became active and we caught 13 good brown trout in an hour. I trade shots with Danny, partly because I've loved to row since childhood, and partly because I like to watch a fine angler in action. Even when casting in a strong wind he is as perfectly composed as if he were tying his shoes.

One afternoon on the Big Hole I knew we were in for good fishing because a hundred yards downstream an improbable number of swallows and nighthawks were coursing above the stream catching insects. There was even a solitary and rare Clark's woodpecker—the only woodpecker to feed on airborne insects—flying around with his mouth stretched open. Sure enough, when we reached this run the fishing became active with the added delight of being watched by a puzzled infant moose and its mother. We couldn't match the minuscule insects but a small Olive Woolly Worm did the trick for a dozen fine browns.

Looking back at the season I've become calm enough to accept several unpleasant surprises. One day I was annoyed by the fact that we couldn't fish the Jefferson because no shuttle was available in the area to take our car and trailer to the destination point. We ended up on the Lower Madison which is too monochromatic in shape and flow for my tastes. We were blanked the first two hours. It was very hot and windy and I was fantasizing about drinking a gallon of margaritas when I put on an enormous stone fly. Since nothing was happening I wanted at least to see the fly I was casting without squinting through my poor vision. On the first cast a large brown

slashed at the fly and missed and I flopped the fly back in the same place. I had a 5-pound brown trout, the second of my life on a river. (I don't count the huge Lake Michigan browns I have caught whose colors are bleached out until they resemble an Atlantic salmon.) Then minutes later I hooked another brown half again as large which passed near the boat both up- and downstream on separate runs. I guessed the fish to be between 7 and 8 pounds but on its downstream run the fly line was looped around my ankle and we parted ways. Naturally I was pissed, though I recalled losing both tarpon and permit with the same loop around the ankle. A grand fish on the Upper Missouri broke off when my fly line caught on a boot buckle. Another big fish on the Yellowstone slowly encircled a boulder and the leader broke despite my yelling at him not to do so.

I'm a bit too sloppy and diffident to ever reach the level of truly great fishermen. For instance, if fish are hitting tiny tricos I yawn while others tie on size 20 imitations, which I wouldn't see if one were hooked in my nose tip. With occasional success I go in the other direction, tying on an enormous Black Woolly Worm that I call the "dead bat," or a new Orvis fly with the amusing name of Conehead Rubber Bugger. On the Upper Missouri we had no luck with Danny Lahren's hopper invention I named "the divine perineum." I assumed it might work because we had visited a Great Falls strip club the evening before and saw this actual part of the woman's body. If you want to you can check your dictionary. The only fly that worked on the Upper Missouri that violently windy day was a grasshopper imitation the size of the nail on your little finger. This is a spectacular piece of river. One day I saw an uninterested brown that looked like an all-night fire log.

About two months into the season my life evolved into something quite pleasant, a balance I hadn't achieved in a couple of years. Gasps and sobs totally disappeared and when I saw a lawyer or real estate agent I no longer leapt backward screaming like a chimp hit with a cattle prod. In four days of work I would develop stress-related eczema, and then in two days of fishing this skin disease would retreat back into its venomous lair. I'm not saying that trout fishing is a disease cure but that it creates a glorious vacuum where mind and body achieve stability because all the severely nagging problems can't penetrate the mind. For me at least a river can easily overwhelm the piddling problems of near-bankruptcy and a wobbly stock market. Of course back in my studio the bad stuff can emerge from the woodwork mouse holes like baby cobras but at least you know how you can hold them at bay.

With only one month to go in September I stepped up the gas. My friend Peter Matthiessen showed up for our annual two days on the Yellowstone. Unfortunately his arrival was accompanied by the most powerful winds of the season, not to mention a cold wave that chilled the kidneys. This ghastly weather, however, didn't disturb the trout that fed intermittently through-out the day. I tested the middle of the river while Matthiessen hit the banks. I was watching an osprey fight the wind for a meal when I hooked and landed a 5-pound brown. I didn't digest the impact of this until later because the three of us were busy identifying the strange influx of birds along the river. Peter is a grand writer and a naturalist who's taken birding trips simply everywhere in the world. The three of us identified a golden eagle, four bald eagles, a prairie falcon, two peregrines, two Cooper's hawks, two Swanson's, a sharp-shinned, a harrier, and a rough-legged, along with dozens of other species including 50 sandhill cranes that flew low and over our heads. It was boggling. For a change I had to leave most of the rowing to Danny. Trying to maneuver a high-bowed MacKenzie in 50-knot gusts is work for an expert. I recalled us once being caught in a thunderstorm squall that blew down trees and Danny had to jump into the river with the anchor in his arms at our take-out spot. The next access was four hours away and the lightning was giving the air the smell of burned water.

Now, at my cabin in Michigan's Upper Peninsula near Lake Superior I'm speculating on the world problem of what recipe I'll use to cook a grouse and two woodcock for dinner. I've been thinking that it's unlikely I'll be able to afford fifty days in next year's season. I quit writing for Hollywood six years ago but now I'm thinking that one more project could give me another 50 days without a bad conscience. Maybe 75. Why not? It's so good for what ails you. There's the easy camaraderie of fishing with a friend rather than the inevitably contentious atmosphere of working with men on the job. The obvious origin of fishing was in getting food, and maybe the love of this process has become genetic since Pleistocene man dropped a boulder off a cliff onto a river pool full of trout. I'm not going to figure the odds against catching a 10-pound brown but you'll hear about it if I succeed, and I want to do it where I already am rather than catching a plane for New Zealand or Argentina. Maybe life is a succession of trading one obsession for another. I noticed this fall with a waning interest in bird hunting that I was working my dog Rose more often along creeks and rivers so that I could look down long steep banks as if I were an osprey and watch what was happening in the water below.

GETTING SLAMMED

GUY MARTIN

If you are foolish enough to launch a fishing expedition in the Florida Keys armed with a plan, you will not keep it for long. There may be a way to blame the sun, the rain, the wind, or the tackle, but there is a force larger than the particulars in this wilderness that breaks down human endeavor. The Keys are an extremity, like outer space. Nothing is supposed to work here. Nothing often does.

On the seagrass meadows, or flats, of the mangrove islands on the northern flank of the Keys live the tarpon, permit, and bonefish. These species are the most contrary and arguably the most finicky saltwater gamefish in the world. That they occur in one blessed chunk of wilderness has given rise to what the Keys guides call the Backcountry Grand Slam, or sometimes just "The Triple," meaning that one angler catches each fish of the trinity on a single trip.

Very good flats fishermen can go seasons without a grand slam. Many have just one or two in their lives. It's hard to do with bait; it's even harder to do on a fly, and it's tremendously hard to do in a day. In any event it makes a splendid lifetime angling goal—but it's a very bad idea to go to the keys *thinking* that a grand slam is what you will get. The reason, the flats guides know, is that these fish can hear fishermen think. Despite this, of course, every single fisherman who goes to the flats has a slam in mind, whether he admits it or not.

My group has what I believe is an ideal plan for a Backcountry Grand Slam, or at least a plan that the fish won't be able to decipher; namely, no plan at all. The heart of our strategy is the humble boat trailer and the even more modest trailer hitch. With it, we are going to take the war to the fish, ranging up and down the lower Keys, putting in here one day, there the next, according to the vast catalog of flats and tides in Capt. Bruce Chard's sun-baked head. The fish will never know what hit them. It's our way of not telling them what we're going until we do it.

"Every 2 miles north in the ocean is an hour later in the tide," says the affable Chard, who, at 32, has been guiding in the lower Keys for the last eight years. "Sometimes they like a little water on the flat, sometimes they like a *lot* of water on the flat, and some flats fish better for bones or permit rather than both. But the big thing is current: no current, no fish."

What Chard means is that, in a sturdy, 18-foot flats skiff that tops out at 45 miles an hour and draws just 12 inches of water, we can chase the tide changes north, or put ourselves at an angle to the tides and chase them east or west, increasing our access to a variety of flats at their best time of day. It does not mean that the fish will oblige us by taking our flies or bait. It does mean that we can fish many different places where they might.

With his sun visor barely containing his sun streaked ponytail, Chard looks like a University of Florida upperclassman who has wandered off the Phi Delta Theta party raft, but he fishes so well that the Teeny Company is developing a permit fly line in his name. We also have a live well full of crab and shrimp in case the wind, or the fish, won't let us fish with flies.

Our second boat is captained by Mike Sobr, a fisherman out of Sarasota. Sobr's boat is a prototype—a Panga flats boat, built in Mexico. It's beamier than the classic Keys skiff, but at 21 feet long still only draws about 10 inches of water, fully loaded. Sobr's angler will be photographer and Montana trout aficionado Dusan Smetana.

This cast of characters is thinking big. At 6 A.M. war council over scrambled eggs and grits, we decide to go to the Marquesas, a wilderness atoll 30 miles west of Key West, to fish for permit. The Marquesas are nothing but a tangle of busy mangroves formed in a great necklace of green islets around a submerged limestone hilltop, but this hill lies in the middle of the ocean, miles from anywhere.

Inside the Marquesas is a pristine 2-mile-by-2-mile seagrass meadow. Such fields are the habitat for the crustaceans that are the diet of bonefish and permit. Because this atoll's inner bay is sheltered, and because of offers such rich food, many larger species use the meadow for breeding grounds. Crucial to the equation is the turtle grass. More than 30 species of tropical invertebrates depend on the grass, which is the absolute rock upon which the food chain of the Keys' $34 million annual sport-fishing industry rests. The meadows of the Keys, including the big one inside the Marquesas, form the largest seagrass bed in the world.

The Marquesas are an aquatic Mojave. One dresses to fish them as one dresses for the desert: long sleeves, long pants, nose masks, kepis. As the backcountry of the backcountry, the Marquesas have for decades exerted a strong pull on the fishermen of the Keys. Hemingway took John Dos Passos there on a fishing trip in 1929. A snapshot of the two writers on that trip is framed in Hemingway's dressing room in the old Whitbread Street house in Key West. In it, both men stand on the great sea meadow in long pants, with no fish, wet to their knees.

Chard and Sobr blast their boats out of Key West harbor, bound to fish Hemingway's flat. At Boca Grande Key, we hit the big channel water coming off the Atlantic, and Chard's 18-footer vaults into the air from swell to swell like an oceangoing dope runner. The only way to take it is to stand up and hang onto the console rail. Chard calls this a "calm" crossing, then smiles a little wicked smile.

At the atoll, we pass quietly through a cut between keys to Mooney Harbor, a 7-foot-deep piece of water in the southern quadrant of the great Marquesas meadow, and enter the grand amphitheater of fish. Waxy green mangroves surround us. Chard noses the boat north, to a big flat inside the elbow of the northern Marquesas. It is a white-hot day. There are no humans here except for us.

We begin by baitfishing with crab on 8-pound-test. On a fly rod or on spinning rigs, the angling routine in these skiffs is like 19th-century whaling on a small scale. The guide is elevated on his platform over the motor. Rod in hand, the angler stands at the ready on the foredeck, exactly as the 19th-century Cape Codders stood ready to harpoon whales. The difference is that whales are a whole lot easier to see than permit.

Sobr and Smetana work the eastern side of the meadow. Chard works west, parallel to the mangrove shore. I stand, shifting my weight from foot to foot, ready to cast.

A lemon shark lazes by. Lemons are bone and permit predators, so he's good to see. Then life, which is to say, everything on the meadow, seems to sag. Chard sniffs the air and calls it: We're moving to a different section of the flat. I muse on the shimmering knowledge of guides, how they have brains that actually think like fish. I reel in, stow my rod, and turn to the console, and there stands Chard, line shooting off the back of his boat, his reel emitting the low moan of being punished by a large fish. It's our permit.

Chard can't pole and fight at the same time. He hands the rod to me. I jump on the foredeck as he jumps back on his poling platform to dress the nose of the boat into the fish.

"He came from behind," Chard says, shrugging coolly. He's got a blisteringly fast cast. His friends call him Wyatt Earp, for his quickness on the draw.

Permit fight like truck drivers whaling on you with tire irons. Specifically, permit are huge pompano and thus are richly muscled, with a deep V tailfin cut for heavy pulling. They're fast, but the runs are not as electric as those of a bonefish. Instead, they use their huge lateral muscles to try to pull you in the water, or break your leader, or yank the rod out of your hands, whichever comes first.

This one is pulling my line out on the port side of the boat. He's got 90 feet of it already, and he's curling around like a mule for another go. I can feel his back working. He runs aft, then crosses to the starboard side. Sometimes, the fish I fight remind me of certain people because of the quality of the battle. This permit reminds me of Secretary of Defense Donald Rumsfeld beating up a pack of reporters at a Pentagon press conference. Every time I drill down on him, he sets his jaw, adjusts his glasses, and smacks me back.

Ten long minutes later, I've got the honorable secretary tuckered out, but before he submits, he tries to run under the Panga in a last effort to put a shadow between him and me. I work him out from under the boat, and we land him. He's 20 pounds, a big one—blue and liquid gold and glorious as the wild Marquesas sun.

"Dude," says Chard, "We are Marq-i-*fied*."

At six the next morning, we're back fishing off Little Torch Key, poling along a flat right next to the Atlantic, fishing for bones on fly rods. The permit have—clearly—telepathically radioed from the Marquesas to tell the bonefish not to show up for us here. There is nothing on this flat; even the ubiquitous cormorants have evaporated. In the distance, we can see Smetana on the upswept prow of Sobr's Panga casting his spinning rod once in awhile. But to what? In an hour, they motor over.

"Let's get out of here," Chard says to them.

"Uhh, we saw maybe five groups of five bones, couple of permit," says Sobr, diplomatically. "They were coming up on the other side."

It's a classic Keys moment. The boats are on the same flat, 200 yards apart. One has multiple shots at serried pods of fish. The other gets skunked.

Still, we decide to shoot north into some better tides and some tight mangroves. A quick 12-minute run at hyperspeed, and we're in a different aquatic arena, farther from the ocean, more vegetated. Some of the mangroves are so close that you have to lift your back cast to clear them.

"Dude! Behind me!"

I whip back to face him. Chard wants me to cast *around* his pushpole at a bone some 30 feet off the back of the boat. I throw a sidearm shot that snakes past Chard. The cast wasn't horrible, a bit to the left, maybe. I strip. The bonefish doesn't spook so much as he collects his hat and cane and saunters off.

It's midafternoon, and the heat bears down on the flats with physical weight. Chard and I bonefish, because we are men, and because we caught a permit, making the next thing on our grand slam list a bone. We pole through tight mangroves near Big Torch Key.

Smetana and Sobr have been working a rank of mangroves about a hundred yards east. We don't see them for long stretches, but then we hear a strange humanoid bark in the trees, and they heave into view. Smetana is standing stiffly over his spinning rod, fighting something.

"Bowwwwne!" Sobr hollers over the water at us.

We pole over to the party. Bonefish can sprint, thrash, and shake across a flat at 30 miles an hour, which gives them plenty of time to wrap a line around a sea fan or a rock and cut it, especially early on, before you have worn them down. Smetana works this bone for 10 minutes and then calls the fish to heel. He's a hefty 9-pounder.

Smetana dances around the foredeck of the Panga in a sort of ugly Czech disco-man dance. "I caught my first bone!"

"Excellent," says Chard.

It could never be the real thing, but it's our two-thirds of a haphazard, two-boat, four-angler grand slam: a start, a seedling of a shadow of an accomplishment. Just the fact that Smetana's catch is a slam species gives it a shard of reflected glory, like fools' gold. This is just the barest taste of the siren song that makes fishermen all over the world want to go for the real deal.

Since we have had no plan for our grand slam—but are, in fact (in a fake way), en route to one—we are forced to admit that we now have a goal and must fish accordingly. We must flyfish for tarpon. This is perhaps foolish, but, like everything else in this place, maybe not.

Early on our third morning, we put the four of us in the Panga and run to Howe Key. The tarpon are in a bridge season, which makes things tough. The big migratory fish are gone, but what the guides call "baby" tarpon, 50-pounders who will stay and grow here for a season, are fishable in some north backcountry mangroves.

Five minutes after we reach the flat, we spot three baby tarpon rolling 200 feet off the port side. Mike Sobr takes the Panga's foredeck. Chard poles to boat to the right. Sobr throws a sharp, pretty loop that lands 60 feet off the port bow. There's a small suck and rustle in the water as one of the tarpon turns to the fly. Sobr bends to strip, but it takes him a second to adjust his posture, and the tarpon noses off to his brothers.

"Dude," says Chard, consoling him.

There are big tarponlike thunderheads, thousands of feet tall, jousting at each other 20 miles east of us. Now, instead of fishing, *we* are being fished by the storm. We pole up the flat for another 20 minutes, but the tarpon have gun.

"The storm's flattened them," says Chard.

The thunderheads' march brings rain just east of us, a gray wall walking. Chard's fly rod begins to vibrate with the electric charge preceding the storm. These are the seeker charges for lightning. Keys guides say this is a sign from the gods when they want to kick you off the water.

"Waterspout," says Chard. "Back east."

Waterspouts are the most surreal, and fitting, expression of Keys weather. The thunderheads literally suck up a column of water a couple of hundred yards tall, a baby tornado, but made of the sea. Water shouldn't, by rights, flow up to the sky, but here, it does.

One shot at a baby tarpon, less than a half day on the water, and God's boot.

Bonefish will eat before bad weather—in fact, they eat well, Chard says, but tarpon get put down by it. Here we are part of the grand wheel of weather, tide, and wildlife: At this level of play it makes no sense to blame the small things such as the rain. There is a force larger than the particulars in this wilderness that breaks down human endeavor; the trick, if you are human, is to try to swim along with it, and be the best that you can be. Nothing is supposed to work here, except what wants to work. This is why, in the Keys, you may wake up thinking that you will be doing something that day, and a few hours later find yourself doing something entirely different.

We gun the Panga down the long storm verge, trying to outrun it. Five miles south is a sliver of sunlight on the bridge to Little Torch Key. The raindrops get fatter and thicker and beat straight into our eyes. Then the storm has us racing blind.

ON THE ROAD
IN BASS PARADISE
JOHN MERWIN

It was an idea born in a January snowstorm. Fed up with shoveling snow, I went inside, logged on to the Internet, and started checking out the perfect antidote to a severe Northern winter: a Southern bass fishing trip. The digital photos of big largemouths from Texas and Southern California that scrolled up my screen were all Florida-strain monsters. And that decided it for me. After all, what better place to catch a Florida largemouth than in Florida, where it all began?

I'd fished here and there in the state over the years, mostly along the coasts where the inshore fishing was as good as the coastal development was ugly. The main routes have been strip-malled and condo-ed into a kind of homogeneous oblivion. Not only does everything look more or less the same, but it also looks like Mountain Home, Arkansas, and Burlington, Vermont, and every other American town where any sense of place has been buried under acres of asphalt and look-alike chain stores.

Florida has about 7,800 lakes, most in its interior and most with bass. That's more than any other state south of Wisconsin. The interior, too, is home to the timber industry, the huge citrus growers, and vegetable farms and cattle ranches. There'd be some space there, I reasoned, some room where I could both fish for bass and breathe deep of the country. The fishing would be more about eyeballing a wild alligator near the boat or marveling at the grace of an egret, or so I hoped, than it would be about fighting traffic. I wanted, somehow, to get to the soul of the thing.

So I called a fishing friend, Don Lewis of Jacksonville, Florida, to suggest a bass fishing tour of Florida's heartland. Yes, he had a week off at the end of March, he said, and we worked out the lakes and the routes and the schedules amid the trials of earning our respective livings. We'd have six days on the road, hitting five major lakes in as many days. This is what we found.

After a long haul down Interstate 95 from the Jacksonville airport, Lewis and I finally pull in to a Best Western Motel west of Vero Beach on a Saturday night. I am not happy.

"I know this isn't the 'real' Florida you had in mind," Lewis says as he eases the boat trailer back into a spot fronting our rooms. "But it's what there is. Stick Marsh–Farm 13 is pretty remote, and there's no place closer to sleep. But don't worry. It gets better." I am exhausted from a long day's travel, and sleep the sleep of all anglers on the night before, restless and dreaming of fish.

Stick Marsh–Farm 13 has been one of the country's hottest bass lakes almost since its creation in 1987. Enclosed by levees and water-flow gates and controlled by one of Florida's several water-management districts, it covers about 6,500 acres. The Stick Marsh portion contains standing timber with numerous tree stubs just below the surface; the adjoining Farm 13 area is a flooded vegetable farm. It's all prime bass habitat, managed as catch-and-release only, and famous for double-digit largemouths.

The next morning is cool, clear, and sunny—a great day for fishing but not so great for catching. Grayer and warmer would be better. We gas up the truck and boat at yet another convenience store, grab sandwiches and bottled water for the cooler, and head west. The roads and towns both get smaller as we travel inland. Eventually we crawl over 6½ miles of rough dirt road heading north and west through a vast expanse of fascinating noth-ingness. Birds suddenly abound, from the flashy white of cattle egrets to the anonymity of sparrows, and the plants and trees expand to an infinite variety. This is more like the Florida I'd hoped to see.

Finally there's water, and a boat ramp, and we're fishing. Back in a corner of the Farm 13 section, a bass nails my topwater prop bait twitched in an open alley among the hydrilla beds, and I unhook a 2-pounder while keeping an eye on the alligators that dot the shoreline. Lewis scores quickly, too, with a similar-size fish on a pumpkin Zoom Trick Worm, Texas-rigged and lightly weighted.

"So, what do we got going on this?" he asks, releasing the fish with a splash.

It takes me a minute. Then I remember that Lewis is very active in local and regional bass club tournaments. "Look," I say, "I don't fish tournaments. I don't even bet. I just like to fish."

He frowns. "We've gotta have something."

"Okay, let's do this," I propose. "One drink after fishing each day. For size, not for numbers. Loser buys the round." It's his water, after all, and there's no way I'll beat him on numbers. With dumb luck, though, I might get the day's big fish.

"You're on." He laughs but starts casting harder. "C'mon, baby," he says to his plastic worm. "Get me a margarita fish."

The action in the bright sun is slow: a fish here on a worm, another there on a Rat-L-Trap, none of them very large. At last, I drop an unweighted 5-inch Senko in a hydrilla pocket, watch the line make a sharp twitch, and set the hook in what turns out to be a 4½-pounder. I give Lewis a good look before releasing it.

Our new-lake-every-day schedule doesn't leave time for much. By nightfall, we've hauled the boat south and west to the north shore of Lake Okeechobee and checked in to another motel. Soon I'm wrapping myself around a very good steak at the Brahma Restaurant in downtown Okeechobee. The margaritas, meanwhile, cost Lewis 10 bucks, and I apologize profusely through several toasts for catching the larger fish.

At about 730 square miles, Lake Okeechobee is probably the world's biggest bass pond. It's very shallow—15 feet deep at most—and surrounded by marshland and weedy edges that are home to tens of thousands of bass.

This morning is clear and cool, and we've run out of the Kissimmee River mouth past an army of crappie anglers and into the main lake. Wind here can be a huge problem. With its long, open reach, it can seriously kick up the big water. Today it's blowing out of the northwest. Our 20-foot Ranger can handle the chop, but it's obvious that we'd get the crap beat out of us if we tried running to any distant hotspot. So we take a quick cut into the nearest lee shore, which happens to be Eagle Bay and Grassy Island in the northwest corner. In this huge area, there's only one other boat in sight—not bad for one of the world's best bass lakes.

One of the reasons I've buddied up with Lewis, aside from his being a good guy, is that he's a professional forester who for 17 years was the director of the forest technology program at Lake City Community College west of Jacksonville. I figured that anybody who ran a forest-ranger school for that long could tell me a lot about regional ecology. And so I learn this morning that those clumps of tall, slim reeds in the water are bulrushes (known as buggywhips) and the low, dense clumps of plants that look like lily pads stuck in the air are spatterdock. And yes, that's eelgrass under the surface in the more open water. There are some bass amid the buggywhips and eelgrass. But there are more back in the narrow channels amid the spatterdock.

Then I get a fishing lesson. One of Lewis' pet lures is a Rat-L-Trap, and he's tossing a ¼-ounce version down the open alleys. He keeps it moving fast and shallow with a high-rod retrieve, snapping the rod sharply when he feels the lure hitting the tops of emergent hydrilla below the surface. That keeps it from clogging with weeds and simultaneously pops it into a new section of open water. He is nailing bass with this technique almost faster than I can count them. They are mostly small but bass nonetheless.

"I could switch to a bigger ½-ounce version," he explains, "and maybe pull a larger fish. But I'd get hung up a lot more often, and I don't know if that's worth it." He zips another cast up another small channel and nails another bass. I sit and eat a sandwich. There's a mature bald eagle soaring far off, its white head and tail distinct against a sky growing gray. Out in the main lake, a big gator cruises slowly and deliberately at the surface, heading with the wind toward some distant shore.

We still have miles to go this day, wanting to make Henderson's Fish Camp on Lake Istokpoga before dark. So, all too soon we're pulling the boat, then bumping our way north through the countless traffic lights on

Florida Route 27 toward Sebring. Lewis had the margarita fish today, of which he reminds me several times as we finally pull up at Woody's BBQ in Lake Wales, which is close to home for the night. Okay, okay; I'll pay up. Ah ha! Drinks on special: 99 cents. My pay-off bar tab comes to $2.12. Lewis feels grossly gypped, but I'm all smiles.

Florida's bass fishing tradition extends as far back as naturalist William Bartram's narratives of exploration here in the 1700s. In modern form, though, the sport didn't take off until the growth of rail travel years after the Civil War. By the early 1900s, Florida was the bass fishing playground of such notables as James Heddon, generally credited with being the inventor of the wooden bass plug. Heddon's first lure catalog appeared in 1902 and featured a photograph of his son Will with a stringer of huge Florida bass.

Today the last vestiges of that history are found in the old-time fish camps common to many larger Florida lakes. I wanted to stay in just such a place on Istokpoga and had picked Henderson's Fish Camp near Sebring at random on the Internet.

At the end of a late-day haul up from Okeechobee, we finally pull to a stop in a grove of live oaks at Istokpoga's edge. Long fronds of Spanish moss wave gently from the tree limbs, shading several small, white cabins. A few boats are sitting on the grassy bank nearby. The whole thing looks like a movie set from the 1950s. One small building has a sign that says OFFICE, and I enter it.

A young girl sits astride a wooden stool on one side of a low wooden counter at one end of the room, and as I watch, she carefully picks out two candy bars. Opposite her, an older man with a grizzled chin and twinkling eyes totes up the purchase with all due care and deliberation. It's a serious moment and not to be interrupted. So I look around at the few mounts of monstrous bass on display, the bits and odds of tackle for sale, the faded pictures of fish gone by, the cooler and the coffee pot. I'm very quickly right at home.

The kid finally flounces out the door the way young girls do. I say hello and give my name and yes, we have a reservation, and yes, I understand it's cash. Terry Trimble scratches out a simple receipt in pencil. No key. Don't need one, he says, but you can lock it if you want. Our particular cabin is an older two-bedroom trailer—clean and everything works—with a screened porch and a rocking chair. Seventy-five bucks a night for two guys: perfect.

Mabel Henderson, whom I meet an hour later, runs this bit of heaven. She's a slight, friendly woman who could be anybody's favorite grandmother. There is, I'm sure, a spine of steel behind her sweet smile. It is not easy running a fish camp, and she's been managing this one since 1975. She'd been a hairdresser in Indiana, she tells me, coming here on vacations with her husband, when they finally convinced the former owners to sell. Her husband died a few years back, and now she and Dennis Rutledge, her son-in-law, keep the place going. She likes to fish, bass sometimes but mostly specks (black crappies), which Istokpoga has in great abundance. She offers laughter and the promise of coffee at 6:30 a.m.

Lewis doesn't know this lake well, and he's called on one of his buddies—Gerald Batten, who happens to be vice president of the Florida Bass Federation—to drive over from Naples to show us around. I've just gotten my morning cup when Batten rolls in, and we launch our boats on Henderson's paved ramp. The early fog is thick at first, and we idle carefully out the channel to the 28,000-acre main lake. Wading blue herons are everywhere, popping eerily in and out of the mist and croaking their displeasure as we pass.

The fog is starting to break, and we can run on plane. We stop at a large island surrounded by acres and acres of buggywhips in the water. Today's drill, Batten tells us, is flipping the whips. So we Texas-rig straight-tailed plastic worms with light weights at the nose, because ones with curled or ribbon tails would tangle and grab too much in the heavy cover. Green pumpkin, watermelon red, and black are hot colors as we slowly cruise the edges, tossing the worms into the thick stuff and gently twitching them back between the upright plant stems. The bass are hitting fairly well but are running only 1 or 2 pounds.

I'd gotten a hot tip on the quiet from one of my new buddies back at Henderson's, and Batten graciously agrees to follow my advice. We run the boats across the big lake to a particular landmark (sorry—secret) and start fishing by the same method. Batten, who has by now worked his way far

back into the buggywhip thickets, shouts, and we hear a loud splashing. Then a long silence. "She was a real horse," Batten says, groaning. "I hooked her and she started going straight up a tight clump of whips. Twisted the hook out."

Inspired, I rig one of the same Senkos that scored a bigger fish at Farm 13 two days before, and drop it into a small opening among the whips. The line gives a telltale quiver, and I set the hook on 4½ pounds of bass, which makes me very happy. I kick back with a honey bun and some water. Lewis keeps casting but takes only a couple more small fish. I softly sing a few lines from "Margaritaville."

We have another lake to make, and so it's another short day. Once again we are bumping our way in the late afternoon up Route 27, headed for the northern end of Lake Kissimmee about 40 miles from Orlando.

As it turns out, my big fish today is partly for naught because the restaurant we eat at tonight has no bar. Lewis owes me one.

I am about as grumpy this morning as I ever get. Last night we checked into another fish camp—also one I chose online—near the north end of Kissimmee. The place is truly a dump, as depressing as Henderson's was cheerful. The icing on this moldy cake is in the shower stall, where the water-control knob is missing. In its place is an old pair of rusty pliers with which to work the stub of a shower control. By the rust stains on the bathtub, the pliers have been a fixture for a long time. All for $100 a night, with an additional $10 cash for a key deposit, and $5 more for every boat to be launched on their ramp—this is money grubbing at its worst.

"Well," Lewis says and smiles. "You wanted a funky old fish camp. This is it." The moral: Always check any kind of no-name lodging as carefully as you can ahead of time.

Kissimmee is a drop-dead gorgeous lake that helps to shake off my ill humor. At 40,000 acres, it's also a good example of Florida's newly enlightened trends in bass-lake management. Because big lakes here are fertile and shallow, they accumulate lots of dead and dying plant material on the bottom over time. New crops of water plants grow rapidly, too, sometimes choking off portions of a lake, which harms spawning success.

In 1996, Kissimmee was drawn down to partly dry out and kill some of the overly dense shallow-water plants. At the same time, some areas were scraped and scooped with heavy equipment to remove accumulated muck and thereby create both better spawning habitat and easier shoreline access when the lake level was again raised. This sort of treatment, in addition to aggressive catch, size, and/or slot limits on some lakes, is the kind of management that's now producing a dramatic resurgence in the quality of Florida's bass fishing.

Not that you could prove it by our luck on this particular morning. We are fishing perfect bass cover that stretches nearly out of sight: big patches of spatterdock interspersed with narrow alleys of open water, a few stands of buggywhips, and cattails here and there. Fish are breaking occasionally in the early light. But we can't buy a bass, which is pretty pathetic for a couple of hotshots.

We manage to hit just a few over the next couple of hours—some on topwaters in the alleys but mostly by flipping the whips as we'd done on previous days. Our results are nothing spectacular but respectable.

Near dark, we're back at the shack. Today's margarita fish belongs to Lewis, but again, the only restaurant around doesn't serve. Our running bet becomes—temporarily—a wash. The next morning we'll head north at 5 a.m. for a day of shiner fishing on Rodman Reservoir south of Jacksonville.

Rodman Reservoir is a 9,500-acre minefield of submerged trees, standing timber, floating stumps, and thick vegetation that's primarily navigable only by an old barge channel running more or less down its middle. The lake has had a huge national reputation for big bass almost since it was built in 1968 as part of a now defunct boondoggle called the Cross-Florida Barge Canal.

It's still controversial. Various environmental groups are fighting to get the dam removed and restore the Ocklawaha River as a free-flowing tributary to the St. Johns. Fishermen, including bass anglers nationwide, are fighting to keep the dam and the spectacular fishing that Rodman provides. In recent years, it's become a political stalemate. The state Legislature has refused to appropriate money for dam removal. But the governor recently vetoed a bill that would have preserved it. Rodman's future is uncertain. If you want to fish it, don't wait too long.

Two more of Lewis' bass buddies, George Deckman and Larry Maurer, meet us at the boat ramp and stock our live well with big golden shiners. We follow them gingerly through a narrow path threading the submerged timber into a more open sort of back bay near shore. Here we each slow-troll a live shiner about 3 feet under a bobber. The boat moves into the wind on its trolling motor, at an unhurried crawl that keeps the shiner moving naturally. The water explodes under Lewis' bait and a 4-pounder goes airborne. He releases the fish and baits up again.

Shiners are the best way to move really big fish, and I track my bobber with years of anticipation riding on that hunk of foam. There's a huge, shocking splash right behind my bobber. I yell and start to set the hook in the mother of all bass. Then in horror I see the flapping wings of an osprey rising from the foam, and it flies skyward with my shiner in its talons.

The bird drops my bait. Lewis is doubled over laughing. Behind us I see three more ospreys circling low, eyeballing all the shiner sets. For the next hour, we have osprey wars: birds diving on the baits, fishermen yanking them away. We finally discover that when an osprey stoops and dives on a particular bait, jerking and splashing the bobber makes the bird flare off.

We give up eventually, and the birds do, too. Instead we still-fish, anchored in a pocket of timber. By luck or good grace we've managed to set up on a pod of hot fish, and the action is nonstop. At first, the bobber is nearly motionless as the shiner I've rigged swims quietly. Then I can feel it getting excited as the baitfish and bass spot each other. Stalking bass create big swirls near the surface; at other times, the bobber jiggles wildly and then goes down, deep and fast. Hard, swift strikes avoid gut-hooking the bass, and one such sweep of the rod puts a 7-pounder in the net for me. It's not the biggest we might have caught, to be sure, but still our record for the week, and I give it a war dance on the front deck.

That night back in Jacksonville, I get another margarita courtesy of Lewis. It represents my third winning bass in five days of fishing, and I'm secretly quite proud of myself. For a gnarly old Yankee in Bubba-land, I haven't done half bad.

Lewis and I part at the airport the next morning. I pronounce him an all-around great guy and fisherman. He pronounces me an honorary redneck. It is, ironically, the second of April, the date in 1513 that Spanish explorer Ponce de Leon discovered Florida and vainly searched for a fountain of youth. It's too bad he didn't discover Florida's bass fishing instead, a true source of everlasting wonder.

BAJA BY BIKE
NATE MATTHEWS

There's a sheet-metal figure of the grim reaper that stands on a highway in the mountains just south of Mulegé, about halfway down the Baja Peninsula's eastern coastline. It's an eerie-looking thing, a shrine to a dead traveler, with a scythe in one hand and an owl perched on the other. The owl's eyes are holes punched out of the rusting iron. You can look through them and see dorado breaking bait on the surface of the Sea of Cortez, 1,000 feet below.

I saw the reaper this spring when I passed it with some friends on the eighth day of a nine-day *Field & Stream* adventure spent fishing Baja California, Mexico, by motorcycle. We'd been on the road that day for 10 straight hours and had at least four more to go before we could stop for the night. Our backs were aching; our heads hurt. Chances were good we'd get a shrine of our own if we pushed ourselves much harder.

This trip had been a stretch from the start. A few months earlier I'd convinced myself, my boss, and three of my friends that we could fish our way from San Diego to Cabo and back in just nine days. Four down, three to catch marlin and roosterfish on Baja's East Cape, then a speed run back north, 1,100 miles up Mexico's infamous Highway 1 in time to catch a flight back to New York City. Just to make things interesting, I was doing this without having ridden a motorcycle in my life. I'd crossed the border into Mexico using a learner's permit.

There were two reasons I wanted to visit Baja. First, it has one of the most fertile fisheries left in the world. The Gulf of California, a.k.a. the Sea of Cortez, boils with marlin, wahoo, dorado, and yellowfin tuna. And then there are the roosters, vicious inshore predators that grow to 100 pounds and chase prey right into the surf. They look cool in pictures, and you can catch them from the beach.

Second, Baja is a practical place to have an uncanned adventure. Tickets to San Diego are cheap; the border is only 20 minutes from the airport. If you don't mind eating beans three times a day and sleeping on the beach, you can fish your brains out for weeks without burning up your bank account.

I wanted to fish Baja by motorcycle because: (1) the right bike can get to places on the peninsula most cars can't reach; (2) the riding down there is the stuff of legend; and (3) I figured I'd get a richer sense of the place if I toured it with my head in the open air.

My partners on this trip were my best friend, Kurt Stoddard, adventure photographer Tim Romano, and *Quad Off-Road Magazine* editor Nick Nelson. Kurt is a flight instructor from Lansing, Michigam. We were roommates in college and have been traveling buddies for almost a decade. Tim lives in Boulder, Colorado, and is one of the voices behind the fly-fishing blog on fieldandstream.com. Nick spends a lot of time racing dirt bikes on the Mexican circuit. He was with us as mechanic, translator, and troubleshooter.

Kurt and I were riding Kawasaki KLR650 dual-sport motorcycles, rigged with aluminum panniers to carry our gear and aftermarket exoskeletons to protect the engines if we dumped in nasty terrain. Tim and Nick chased us with the camera in our friend Bill Decker's white Chevy Suburban, which was set up for offroad touring.

The KLR has a nickname that I like; in adventure cycling circles it's known as "The Mule." I thought this was appropriate, since just 30 years before our trip, the only way to access most of the places we were going was by riding a real one.

One of these places was Mike's Sky Ranch, which we made a side trip to visit on our first day. Located deep in the north-central highlands, the San Pedro Mártir Mountains, it caters mostly to Baja's offroad riding community, but it also has a year-round waterway running through its front yard. These are the headwaters of the Arroyo San Rafael, and they spring from high enough up in the mountains to support a rare strain of desert rainbow trout.

You can fish Mike's only if you're skilled (or stubborn) enough to navigate the road to his place. It's about 30 miles long, a rutted-up track through sand and rock that's part of the course of the Baja 500 international offroad race. This is not fun terrain for a novice, especially at the end of a long day on a motorcycle. I crashed once on the way in when my front tire washed out in deep sand, and arrived at the ranch as strung out as I've ever been from traveling.

Fortunately, the place has a well-stocked bar, and the bartender turned out to know a great deal about trout fishing. After we bought a few beers he gave us some tips. Get up early because the heat will drive fish under cover quickly. Walk upstream a few miles to find the best water. The fish would be small. The largest he'd taken in 30 years was just 10 inches long.

In the morning we woke before the sun. I felt like roadkill looks, but I rigged a 2-weight fly rod and grabbed a box of attractors, and we headed up a trail that followed the arroyo. We started fishing where the stream entered a low canyon. Its walls shaded the water, which was cold and woke me up when I knelt in it to thread a cast through the brush. Three drifts later a 5-inch shadow darted from some rushes to swipe my fly. I brought it to hand, admiring the colors. It was a jewel of a trout, more songbird than fish, with white tips to its fins, bold parr marks, and a red lateral line that ran through its eye.

We fished for two more hours, working our way up the river, which was wide enough in places to jump across. I wanted to stay longer but we had a long way to go on the bikes that day; as the sun scared the last of the shadows from the canyon floor, we packed up our rods, hiked out, and hit the road again.

One thousand miles later, we pulled into a small fishing village on Baja's East Cape, about 60 miles northeast of Cabo San Lucas. That we'd survived the trip was something of a miracle; there were all sorts of snares for the unwary *gringo turista*.

One of these was corrupt officials, of which there were two kinds, military and police. Bored teenagers carrying AK-47s manned the military checkpoints, which we hit at most major intersections (there aren't many of these in Baja), and in places where terrain funneled travelers through bottlenecks. At one of them the station's commandant emerged from his gatehouse to check out our bikes and took a liking to my fly rod. He offered to buy it and tried to leverage his bargaining position by flicking off the safety on his rifle. I think I escaped by pleading bad Spanish.

The police might have been worse, but we were fortunate enough to avoid them. Nick said they stop gringos just to take bribes, and he'd brought along a plastic bag full of racing stickers as *mordida*, which translates literally as "the bite." Apparently Baja cops love the things. In case the stickers failed, we never carried all our cash in one place, instead hiding rolls of pesos in our shoes, in side pockets in our bags, and even in rod tubes.

Another hazard was the distance between gas stations. There aren't many towns in Baja, and not all of them sell fuel. Our map marked the ones that did, and we were careful to fill up whenever we saw a pump. But there was one stretch where we had to ride into a nasty headwind, and the extra resistance hurt our mileage so much that by the time we reached the next village we were deep into our reserve tanks. I wasn't that worried until we pulled up to the Pemex station and the pumps were all taped shut. We were saved by an old cowboy selling gas from the back of a cart a bit farther up the road. For a steep fee he siphoned us some juice from one of his oil drums.

Then there were the animals. Cows sleep on the road in Baja after dark, liking the warm pavement. Wild donkeys live in the desert and take on its colors, which makes them nearly invisible. I almost decapitated one when it jumped in front of my bike near San Ignacio. Bugs were an issue when we'd ride through watered areas. Once I had a giant flying beetle smack me in the face when I was cruising along an arroyo at 80 mph. It left a mark on my cheek the size of my palm. Another time a bee flew down my shirt and stung me three times. I almost wrecked trying to clear it from my clothing.

On top of these dangers I worried that we weren't finding enough time to fish. We'd planned our route to follow dirt roads along the peninsula's eastern coastline, adding hundreds of miles to the trip so we could sleep on the beach and fish for a few hours each morning and evening in the Sea of Cortez. But the distances we had to cover, especially on the dirt, took far longer than expected, and each time we got to a campsite the sun was already down. We had barely the time or, frankly, the energy to find a scorpion-free stretch of sand on which to throw our sleeping bags.

At last we had three bike-free days, and I meant to do some serious fishing. We were staying at a place called Rancho Leonero, a sportsmen's resort perched on a bluff of palms overlooking a reef that drops to 1,000 feet just 500 yards from the beach. With a good pair of binoculars you could sit by the pool in front of its bar and glass boats pulling in marlin all day long.

On the first day we hired one of Leonero's 23-foot cruisers, the *Jefe*. We bought live mullet from a bait boat waiting near the dock, then motored out to set our lines. The target was striped marlin, and the rods were thick, like small saplings. They had pulleys in place of guides. We used five rods: two on the outriggers that swung out from the sides of the cabin, one on each corner of the transom, and one in the center of the bridge.

To find marlin you scanned the water, looking for bills and fins breaking the surface, for the splash of a feeding fish, or for one breaching—when the fish would leap 10 feet out of the water, turn in the air, and land with a smack against the surface. Jeff DeBrown, a guide at the resort, told me later that day (Capt. Hermando didn't speak English) that they do this to knock off the lice and remoras that attach to their sides.

A sighting meant pandemonium. "Marleeen! Marleeeen!" Hermando would shout. Jabbing his finger toward the spot where he'd seen it, he'd gun the engine to get our lures ahead of the fish. At times we saw marlin jumping in all directions from the boat. We'd each point at a different fish, screaming *"Allá! Allá! Allá!"* ("There! There! There!"), which gave the captain whiplash. All of us (except for Tim, who was shooting) hooked up at least once. Kurt and Nick both landed 140-pounders; I broke off another after a 30-minute battle.

In the afternoons, Tim and I fished with fly rods for roosterfish from the beach. On the East Cape, beaches consist of parrotfish dung. Parrotfish eat coral, then excrete bits of limestone. Around midday this coral sand gets hot enough to burn your feet.

To catch a rooster from shore you have to spot it, then cast to it, without its seeing you first. This means you walk far back from the waterline, to where the sand is broiling hot, ducking low and looking for shadows in the surf. Every few minutes I had to stop, sit on my butt, and hold my feet in the air to let my soles cool off.

The next day, we took sea kayaks rigged for fishing to the dropoff, where we dunked bait for fish cruising the reef's edge. Our guide was Dennis Spike, a kayak-fishing specialist who rents out boats at Leonero eight months out of the year. We caught lots of triggerfish and some snapper, and Kurt somehow hooked a manta ray on a piece of squid.

Once, when I was live-lining a mullet, something struck it with enough force to knock me off balance and I almost dumped from the boat. The fish dove into rocks and busted me off, my drag useless. Later that day a 12-foot hammerhead swam slowly past my kayak. Spike told me I should have paddled at it to scare it away, to teach it that people aren't something to mess with.

All of this was fun, but my heart was most set on catching a big roosterfish like the 50-pounders mounted on the walls of Leonero's bar. We weren't having any luck doing this from the beach (Tim caught a baby, but that was it), so we called up the *Jefe* again and had Hermando take us near Los Frailes, a point of rocks close to the tiny town of La Ribera, 25 miles southeast along the coast. The scuttlebutt was that monster roosters were busting sardines here 100 yards offshore.

You can catch a roosterfish from a boat in two ways. The first is by chumming live sardines. This was simple: The mate, Rigo, would grab handfuls from the live well, thump them against the transom to scramble their brains, then toss them into our wake. The idea is to tease the roosters into a feeding frenzy and then cast a sardine with a hook in its head into the carnage. The less exciting method is to just troll off the back of the boat, one sardine to a rod, one rod per angler. We held the rods in our hands so that we could react quickly to strikes.

At Los Frailes it didn't take us long to realize we were in the right spot. Roosterfish have a unique dorsal fin called a comb, seven long spines that they erect when they get in a killing mood. Every 15 minutes we'd see new combs break the green surface, cutting white wakes as their owners dashed about and chopped sardines to pieces. These were big roosterfish, working in pairs, and they were smart. We spent all day chasing them around and sticking sardines in their faces without so much as a take.

Toward the end of the day the captain pulled out his secret weapon. On the way down we had purchased our sardines and some odd-looking mullet from two local fishermen selling bait from a small rowboat. The mullet looked odd, I realized, because they were not mullet, but bonefish. I hadn't gotten a good look until Hermando grabbed one out of the live well, stuck a hook through its nose, and handed me the rod.

I asked DeBrown about this later, and he said that using these for bait is relatively normal, and not frowned upon in Baja. The area is full of bonefish but you can't really fish for them because there aren't any flats. Instead the locals catch them in nets and eat them, or use them for bait. They're also a favorite food for roosterfish.

Two big roosters were working off the transom, so I flipped my bone into our wake and let it drift back toward them. One turned, its eyes fixed on the bait, and attacked. When I set the hook, the fish nearly jerked the rod from my hands.

Back in high school I'd once manned the scoring booth at our fire department's annual truck and tractor pull. My job was to record the distances that competitors driving souped-up farm equipment could drag a weighted sled up a loose dirt track. The way this rooster pulled reminded me of one rig I saw there, a rocket-powered tractor that shot 15-foot flames from its pipes. As I held the fish up for pictures, I could feel why. Its flanks were pure muscle, its body as wide and solid as a keg of beer. We estimated its weight at 60 or 70 pounds. Catching it made my trip.

The celebration at the bar that night was muted, because the next morning we had to get on our motorcycles and ride back to San Diego in just two days, half the time it had taken to arrive.

Pushing so hard was a foolish idea. We were already tired from three long days spent battling fish in the sun, and before that the grueling ride down. There would be no breaks, unless we wanted to ride into the night, a very bad idea with those cows on the highway.

Mex 1 is dangerous. It has two lanes and no shoulder, just a bank of sand and gravel steep enough to pull a car off the road. There are few guardrails, even where the road winds through the mountains. *Topes* (speed bumps) and *vados* (sharp dips) are often unmarked, and we saw washouts on the way down large enough to swallow a Volkswagen. Some actually had; we saw corpses of the cars rusting at the bases of cliffs.

But I had set the trip up in part as a test. Too many hours in a New York cubicle had me questioning myself. Could I still handle the hard stuff? Or was I just another desk jockey dreaming behind a computer screen? *If I could bike the Baja like this and live*, I thought, *I could handle damn near anything*. So as the sun came up we rolled back onto the highway, pointed north.

We should have failed, or died. You get careless when you go such long distances without resting. At times I rode almost sidesaddle, hanging my butt off the seat to give it a rest. Kurt's relief position was different; he'd put his feet on the passenger pegs and lean forward until his chest was flat against the tank bag. We pushed the loaded bikes as fast as they could move (my top speed on flat pavement was 97 mph) and still got caught in the dark at the end of the first day, pulling in to the Baja Oasis Motel in San Ignacio at 10 in the evening. When I closed my eyes for the night I could still see the road moving in front of my handlebars.

In the morning we hit the Pacific. The ocean currents along Baja's western coastline flow south from Alaska, bringing cool water to the sun-burned land. This made the air very cold. I wore all my layers and still rode shivering, pressing my legs against the bike to absorb the heat of the engine. A fog lay across the desert, and we traveled north through a forest of shrouded cacti.

But the ride back wasn't all pain, terror, and tedium. On one long stretch of highway just south of El Rosario I realized how much better I'd gotten at handling a motorcycle. It was the afternoon of our last day, and the road was as winding as any I'd seen so far, switchback after switchback, with guardless corners that crumbled into canyons. We banked through miles of the turns, swooping through the mountains and whooping with joy. At the end of the section Kurt pulled into a rare turnout and took off his helmet. His face was glowing. "This," he said, "is where all good bikers go when they die."

Two thousand, three hundred and twenty-one miles. I'd do it again in a New York minute.

RUST-BELT STEEL

JOE CERMELE

Cleveland, Buffalo, and Rochester, N.Y., have two things in common. In the last few years, they have all made various top 10 lists of the fastest-dying cities in America. They are also three of the cities my friend Mark Wizeman and I drove past last November on a 410-mile Great Lakes steelhead fishing road trip. In a region where industry has largely moved away, leaving behind crumbling buildings and abandoned warehouses, the steelhead, one of the most sought-after gamefish in moving water, remains and thrives. We had talked about it for a few years—packing the truck for an eight-day tour of the tributaries that once powered iron foundries and flowed past monolithic grain elevators and humming automobile plants. Like the immigrants that once filled these factories on the shores of the Great Lakes, the steelhead are transplants, too. They will never have saltwater running over their gills, but their fighting ability is no different from that of their West Coast kin. Though their tactics and attitudes vary, the anglers who chase the only steel that hasn't rusted in this part of the country are just as driven.

The faint sunlight showing through a sky dense with cold, gray clouds is about gone. It's difficult to pick out where my fly line meets the water in

the darkened riffle, yet somehow a slight tick registers and suddenly there is a 15-pound steelhead with my egg fly neatly in the corner of its mouth 4 feet out of the water, lunging straight at me. I have hooked seven steelhead in New York's Salmon River today, and landed exactly one a quarter of the size of this fish. I know this will be my last hookup of the day. I'm facing the same obstacles I did with the other six: There are multiple root snarls that this steelhead can run into, and it's pulling against the 4-pound-test tippet necessary to fool these wary trout in the clear water. I am fully aware that the odds are not in my favor as the fish changes direction and tears off downstream. "He just hit go home in his mental GPS," says Gary Edwards with a laugh. "He's going straight back to Lake Ontario." The 59-year-old veteran guide, one of the first ten to ever launch a float boat on the Salmon River, takes off on a sprint downstream with the net as he has thousands of times before in his 30-year career. I have no choice but to follow. My backing is half gone and the fresh chromer isn't about to turn around.

The Salmon is one of the more notorious steelhead rivers on the Great Lakes. Cutting through Pulaski, a town that from the 1840s until recently was home to more than a hundred wood mills, ironworks, and factories, the Salmon River was named for its natural runs of Atlantic salmon. Like the factories and mills, those salmon were largely wiped out after chinook and coho salmon and steelhead were introduced to Lake Ontario in the mid 1960s and became apex predators. That stocking ultimately turned Pulaski into a place where thousands of snaggers lined the banks on Saturdays to throw weighted treble hooks during the fall run, fill coolers, and go home. Many of those salmon were sold commercially, and according to Edwards, the river was rampant with fistfights, petty sabotage, and cutthroat tactics to lock up the best holes and kill the most fish.

Back then, pursuing steelhead largely took a backseat to salmon. Thanks to the illegalization of snagging, as well as guides like Edwards who repainted Pulaski as a destination for conservation-minded sportsmen, and an ever growing infatuation with steelhead, the situation has changed. Pulaski is still economically reliant on anglers. But these days, instead of heavy rods and snag hooks at the tackle shop, anglers are buying Spey rods, shiny Estaz Egg patterns, and tapered leaders at the fly shop.

If there is a visible testament to the attitude shift in Pulaski, it's the

Douglaston Salmon Run—a 2½-mile private stretch of river on the property of former State Sen. Doug Barclay. In the late 1980s, tired of hundreds of blatant trespassers leaving garbage on his property, Barclay, along with guides like Edwards, saw the opportunity to create a new fishery that would weed out the riffraff and take some strain off the highly pressured fish. To fish here you must pay a daily fee, and a limited number of anglers are allowed. There is a strict no-kill steelhead policy, and leader lengths are capped at 48 inches to make it harder for the occasional bad seed to sweep a fly at the end of a run in an attempt to snag.

The move made Barclay Public Enemy No. 1 among local anglers for years. Today, the Douglaston Salmon Run is viewed as a blessing that allows serious fishermen to avoid the shoulder-to-shoulder combat that takes place upriver. Though you can still spot crusty balls of heavy monofilament from decades past wrapped in the trees, the anglers who fish Douglaston are a new breed. There are smiles instead of scowls; advice instead of middle fingers; Orvis waders instead of worn-out rubber hip boots. When Wizeman hooked a fat 12-pound steelie earlier in the day, adjacent anglers considerately moved out of his way and offered congratulations when Edwards sunk the net on it a quarter mile downriver from where it was hooked.

Now Edwards is trying desperately to do the same with my last fish. "Not too much pressure. Turn your rod to the left," he instructs. He is nearly armpit deep, 40 feet downstream in the final shafts of light. We have followed the steelhead for 200 yards, and now it is lolling on the surface but won't let me bring it closer. Then, with a quick headshake, the big steelhead snaps my line and splashes away. Edwards, his net still extended, looks at me and says, "Hey, that was some fight though, wasn't it?"

While strike indicators and nymphs are a key part of a Pulaski fly guide's arsenal, 200 miles west in the quaint town of Lewiston, N.Y., electric fillet knives and Tupperware containers of home-cured egg sacs are standard issue. There are no fly shops on the banks of the mighty Niagara River, no drift boats. Here, there is a fish-cleaning house paid for by the charter fishing association at Lewiston Landing where, every day from September through April, anglers launch beefy Lunds capable of handling the wind chop, vortexes, and extreme currents produced by a deep river moving millions of gallons of water through a relatively narrow gorge every minute. As I help friend and guide Ted Kessler launch his boat, the odor from the cleaning house suggests the steelhead bite has been good.

We are only on the drift for 10 minutes, bouncing brown trout egg sacs freshly dyed hot pink along the rocky bottom on three-way rigs with conventional gear, when Wizeman rears backs. His rod bucks three times, then curls into a deep arc. "Lake trout," Kessler grunts. He can tell the fish isn't a steelie because it's peeling line slowly instead of ripping it away like a greyhound on steroids. A few minutes later, Wizeman brings in a 15-pound laker. We boat three more before Kessler decides there are too many spawning lake trout in the area, and it's going to be a real chore picking through them to hit the steelhead. We move.

Having fished the area his whole life, Kessler is unfazed by the whirling Niagara. At 30 mph, I feel the back of the boat fishtail when Kessler runs over one of the many swirling holes that open and close in the turquoise flow. He tells us it's the Lewiston stretch, where the bodies of most suicide jumpers at Niagara Falls 10 miles upriver eventually resurface. Over our heads, the bridge to Canada is jammed with semitrucks backed up at customs. Ahead, flanking each side of the river, are the 400-foot-high concrete walls of American and Canadian power-generating stations. Strings of power lines create spiderwebs in the cloudless blue sky. Wizeman and I trade concerned looks as Kessler noses the boat into the shooting discharge of the American station a mere 6 feet from the opening of one of the concrete tunnels. "Why are my legs vibrating?" I ask. "That's from the turbines below us," Kessler says, grinning. "You can feel the rumble through the deck. Pretty wild, right, dude?"

There is method to Kessler's madness. The last tunnel in the chain is pumping, but it's spitting out a slower stream of water than the center tunnels. "Every time this one is bubbling, I catch fish," he happily announces as he works the trolling motor to keep us positioned in the slop. Wizeman and I send our spawn sacs down, and it's almost automatic. I get bumped and miss, but Wizeman connects. His drag sings for a few beats, then a hefty steelhead shoots up through the confused white froth, hanging in the air. "Yeah, baby!" shouts Kessler. We get pushed out of the chute and spin wildly for 10 seconds in the main current until Kessler gets control with the big engine. Wizeman's fish is streaking to the bottom and we're all hooting at the chaos. By the time the 10-pounder is in the net, we're a mile downriver. "O.K. Let's get back to the fish factory," Kessler says. For the next three hours, at least one of us ties into a steelhead with each drop into the churning power-plant cauldron.

By sunset, we've probably lost 30 rigs to the jagged bottom of the Niagara, but that's all part of the game. We've also landed 23 steelhead, many of which broke 10 pounds. When we say our good-byes at the ramp, I commend Kessler on his fearless boat handling. "Hey man," he says, "sometimes to get the fish around here, you can't be afraid to rub a little concrete."

"I think it's about time to go make those cookies," Mark DeFrank shouts, a cigarette quivering in his lips. He is sitting on a rock at Elk Creek near Erie, Pennsylvania, in the heart of "Steelhead Alley." Behind him, Wizeman and I stand as still as statues with his partner, guide Chris Kazulen, watching a little lady in sweatpants, sneakers, and a trout vest 30 feet downstream. She is standing on the shale bank in the early sun, trying to lob a nymph under a strike indicator into a short pool black with steelhead. But she can't reach. She told us when we arrived that she was a lunch lady at a local school getting in a few hours of fishing before work, where she'd have to bake six dozen cookies this morning. DeFrank and Kazulen are itching to get at those fish, and polite banter has given way to agitation. They want the run. She knows it, and she's not budging.

Elk Creek is shockingly low and crystal clear from a lack of rain. The bulk of the steelhead that pushed up from Lake Erie at high water are now trapped in the few-and-far-between runs that are at least 2 feet deep. I look up and down the meager flow, which is about 30 feet across at its widest point here. Every so often a steelhead back breaks the surface in the shallows. It looks too easy, but when the cookie lady finally concedes the hole, I learn quickly that I'm wrong.

I step into the water with a tiny size 22 Brassie fly on the end of my 4-pound tippet. My first drift goes untouched. On the next, the little bobber dives. We're all hoping I haven't snagged a fish, which is easy to do when they're this concentrated, but it takes Kazulen only a moment of watching the fight to know I've got it in the mouth. I've found an eater. Problem is, it's a big fish with nowhere to go. For a hairy five minutes I gently keep up the pressure as the ticked-off trout shoots from one end of the pool to the other. If it breaks into one of the 6-inch riffles above or below, I'll lose it. Eventually, Kazulen sloshes into the hole and takes a wild swing with the net. What he comes up with is the biggest steelhead I've ever landed—a glistening female pushing 18 pounds.

Our two guides are like the Laurel and Hardy of Pennsylvania steelheading. DeFrank, a master fly-tier whose steelhead box looks as though it should be propped open under glass in an art gallery, is short and stocky, and gripes about "vultures" (people that cast over your shoulder) and "mup ears" (people from Pittsburgh that "come mup ear" on weekends). Kazulen is tall and lanky, and talks about food incessantly. They bicker like brothers, but between DeFrank's skill at fly selection and Kazulen's eagle eyes, they are a deadly force on the water. At least five times throughout the day, Kazulen will spot lone steelhead in small depressions and riffles that Wizeman and I walk right by.

Thing is, spotting loners and catching them are two different animals. If your first cast isn't dead on, you're going to either spook the fish or snag it. When they do eat, all you get is the slightest head movement to the side, the mouth barely opening wider than when they take a breath. If you had plenty of room to roam and countless chances, it wouldn't be so bad, but miles and miles of Pennsylvania's steelhead creeks cut through private properties, some of which charge anglers to fish, and stretches can book up years in advance. And public water can get busy quickly: As we round a bend, two anglers heading in the other direction tell us not to go any farther. The landowner who usually grants fishermen access is on a bender today and threatening to call the cops on anyone he sees behind the house, because someone left broken beer bottles along the creek.

We return to a pool where we spotted a half dozen fish nervously cruising, and as we're trying to get one to eat, an old man approaches from the bank. He's carrying a beat-up fly rod and reel, and dangling from the end of what must be a straight length of 20-pound mono is a large Woolly Bugger. I count four big split shot only 6 inches above the fly. "Look who it is! Capt. Snag-O-Plenty," Kazulen yells at the man. The old-timer smiles. "Is good fishing?" he asks in a thick Russian accent. When he makes two lobs right between us, we decide it's time to go. "You saw how hard the fishing was today, right?" Kazulen asks me as we walk out. "By the time we get our waders off, he'll be at his car with a limit of fish, you watch."

Later that day we bump into a Pennsylvania Fish and Boat Commission officer at the mouth of Walnut Creek—the state's other noted steelhead tributary. He shows us three homemade snag hooks he's confiscated in the last few days. "It's only Wednesday," the officer says with a sigh. "I'll have a lot more after the weekend."

The next morning, Wizeman and I meet Jeff Kreager in the lobby of our shabby motel in Mentor, Ohio, just east of Cleveland. Kreager, a real estate agent from Newark, Ohio, is a longtime *Field & Stream* reader who comments often on the magazine's website. I knew he had experience in these waters and had asked him to play guide for a day, and he gladly accepted.

Though Kreager admits he is no steelhead expert, his enthusiasm is infectious. "I've never fished this spot before," he says when we pull up to a stretch of the Grand River in downtown Painesville, "but it looks pretty good." There are other flyfishermen walking the trails at the municipal park as we suit up behind Kreager's Jeep, warming up on this cold morning with a nip of peach Schnapps from his flask. We find a quiet pool outside the main current and spread out along the run, each drifting a sucker spawn fly in a different color down the stained Grand.

The water level is good, and everything feels fishy. Even the sudden snow squall that pelts us for 20 minutes signals steelhead. Every time my indicator stops, my heart jumps. But it is our host who finds more than a rock tugging down his float. The big bright female jumps in the center of the pool. Wizeman runs for the net. Kreager takes off downstream behind a fly rod bowed to the brink. "Fighting a steelhead is like fighting a rabbit," he yells over his splashing boots. The three of us are having such a great time that it feels as though we've been fishing together for years. We won't catch another fish after netting Kreager's 12-pounder, but we're all pleased—his steelie is a team victory.

RUST-BELT STEEL

It's about four-thirty when we sit down on the bank, and Kreager opens two tins of Beach Cliff fish steaks in Louisiana hot sauce and doles out coffee from his thermos. We get on a subject other than steelhead, laughing and joking as the Grand flows by. It flows under the highway locked up with commuters heading home from Cleveland, then beneath the railroad bridge in Painesville that once carried train cars loaded with steel and iron ore. Then the Grand will become slow and muddy as it dumps into Lake Erie, where anglers from miles around are hoping a fresh school of steelhead is staging, getting ready to push upstream this weekend.

THE MIDLIFE SLAM

MIKE TOTH

Six miles from land in 8- to 10-foot swells is usually no place to have an argument over a 4-inch fish. But here we are, seven experienced fishermen, heatedly discussing the identity of a little brown-barred creature as the charter boat heaves and yaws, knocking everyone off balance.

"Might be some kind of grunt," says mate K.J. Zeher, grabbing a rod rack to keep steady.

"I don't know." Photographer Ron Modra takes four quick steps sideways as the boat rocks. "Looks like a young grouper."

"You're both wrong," comes the voice from above, not God but one of several apparent close relations I will meet on this trip. This one is Alex Adler, captain of the 48-foot Kalex, looking down from the bridge. Adler has put me onto 15 different species of fish so far today and it's not even lunchtime. "It's a bass. Mike, check your books."

He's right. The fish is a saddle bass, found in 250- to 500-foot depths here off the Florida Keys. There's a scar halfway down its flank—a souvenir from some larger fish beneath us, and there are plenty down there—but the mark didn't throw off Adler, the expert fisherman and, I'm learning, amateur fish taxonomist.

Adler is 50, a milestone age I will reach this year. Like many men of my hairline, I have a family, a job, and a house, all of which demand most of my time and attention. So it might seem that I have better things to do than attempt to remain upright on a rocking boat about 90 miles from Cuba, some of the greatest gamefish in the world swimming in waters around me, preoccupied with a tiny fish wriggling in my hand.

But that is precisely why I am here.

Some men have a so-called midlife crisis when they turn 50. The number is a stark reminder that our lives are well more than half over. Many of us try to deny our fading and failing bodies by buying late-model European sports cars and using pills and ointments in a desperate attempt to retain the same virility, muscle tone, and short-term memory we had in our 20s.

I understood this well-documented reaction to aging on an intellectual level but didn't really feel it until an AARP application arrived in my mailbox earlier this year. I stared at the envelope for a week but didn't dare open it. Just what would be my reward for turning 50? A free large-print book? A discount on an early-bird special dinner at a chain restaurant? Or even (please, no!) The Clapper?

The thought was frightening. No wonder so many 50-year-olds run out to get botulism toxins injected into their face wrinkles and start using the salutation "Dude!" to begin every conversation.

What I wanted to do instead was what had always made me feel right about life—go fishing. A whole lot of fishing. And therein lay a perfect way to mark my 50th: Instead of staring aghast at 50 candles on a birthday cake, I'd spend a week trying to catch 50 different species of fish. It would be an exhilarating way to celebrate an inauspicious birthday, and cheaper than buying a car shaped like a giant Rapala Fat Rap.

To do this I needed a place that wasn't too far from home, where I could spend a week without spending a fortune, where I'd have access to docks and boats and guides and a lot of water, so I could spend as much time as possible fishing. And, of course, where I'd have a realistic chance of catching 50 species.

The Florida Keys, a 125-mile island chain extending from the southeastern tip of Florida, seemed the ideal destination. The Keys have an incredible abundance of fish. There are billfish and dolphin a quick run offshore, bonefish and tarpon on the sandy flats, redfish and seatrout in the backcountry region, plus snapper and grouper and jacks and scores more species—various sources put the number at 400 or 500, total. No one knows exactly how many; maybe whoever started to count them got caught up in the great fishing and said to hell with the project.

It was a fail-safe plan, because if I didn't catch the 50, I'd still be spending a week in fishing paradise. With no flaming cake to look at.

In Carl Hiaasen's novel *Stormy Weather*, Clinton Tyree, the itinerant and partially deranged ex-governor of Florida, has himself lashed to the railing at the apex of the Card Sound Bridge in order to witness a hurricane heading toward south Florida. As I drive over that bridge this late June day I don't even see a cloud, just an expanse of brilliant blue water extending alongside and beyond Key Largo.

This bridge is one of two vehicle-accessible entries to the island chain. U.S. 1, the Overseas Highway, connects the Keys, which are formed of limestone outcroppings capped by ancient fossilized coral. Some are developed, some are not. Some are so narrow that you can stand in one spot and see both the Gulf of Mexico and the Atlantic Ocean, which the Keys—there are about 800 of them—essentially separate.

My destination is Upper Matecumbe Key and the village of Islamorada (EYE-la-more-AH-duh), about a third of the way down the island chain. Islamorada bills itself as "The Sportfishing Capital of the World," and few argue the designation. Fishing boats bristling with rods occupy every dock—a wild array of party boats, offshore sportfishing boats, flats boats, cuddy cabins, walkarounds, and center consoles. Mounts of king mackerel and permit and marlin hang not just in tackle shops but in motels, restaurants, bars, and gas stations. Some are outside, so that you can see giant tarpon and great white sharks without leaving your car.

By the time I pull into Cheeca Lodge, my home for the next seven nights, it is near sunset. Cheeca is a large and beautiful resort on the Atlantic side. I am staying at this famous lodge, which I'll only see early mornings and evenings, because my family will be joining me later in the week (my wife had eight words to say about my adventure—"You're not going to the Keys without me"—and she and the kids will enjoy the swimming and the snorkeling here while I'm out on the water).

I've been traveling all day but I have fish to catch. So after checking in, I grab my rod and walk past the swimmers in the lagoon and the pool, past the outdoor restaurant. I ignore the calypso music emanating from the speakers in the palmettos and the quiet hum of a piña colada blender at the tiki bar. I resist all these temptations because of the other main reason I'm staying at Cheeca—a 525-foot-long fishing pier on the property.

I walk to the end and bait up with shrimp I bought at the Worldwide Sportsman across U.S. 1 from Cheeca. Looking down, I see a kaleidoscope of small fish, along with a 12-foot nurse shark cruising lazily around the pilings. I cast, and the shrimp flows with the tide for only a few seconds before I feel a sharp rap. I set the hook and shortly bring up an 8-inch light-colored fish with yellow lateral lines, a gray spot two-thirds back, and small, sharp teeth. I take a photo and drop it back into the water. Later that night my reference books will show that species No. 1 is a lane snapper, a common and good-tasting species.

With a dozen more fish, I add three more species—pinfish, margate, and bluestriped grunt—to my list. It's well after dark now and I'm tempted to keep going, but 50-year-olds on a mission (who've been up since 4 a.m.) need their sleep.

The next morning I'm at Robbie's Marina, a five-minute drive from Cheeca. Robbie's is the home of the Captain Michael, a 65-foot party boat, as well as rental boats, snorkeling and diving services, and a huge school of giant tarpon that are being hand-fed baitfish by tourists at the end of a dock.

I watch the show until the boat leaves. Our destination, according to Capt. Ron Howell, is a reef 3½ miles from shore on the ocean side, where we'll go after yellowtail snapper.

The boat can hold 53 people, and we are about half full. We cross under U.S. 1 at the Indian Key Channel Bridge. I marvel at the various hues of the water—azure, turquoise, emerald—that change with depth and bottom composition.

We reach the reef 3 miles out. Howell circles it while mate Marshall Hill puts out chum bags. We anchor and drift our baits into the slick. I'm fishing a squid strip on a $\frac{1}{16}$-ounce yellow jig. A school of sublegal dolphin—"chickens"—shows up, and one grabs my bait. There are bigger dolphin farther offshore, but on this trip, size doesn't matter. It's species No. 5.

The yellowtail show up in the chum slick, their golden tails flashing, but they're not biting well. "The water's too clear," says Howell. "They're spooky." Hill has me change to a No. 4 bait hook with a small strip of ballyhoo, a baitfish common to these waters, and I'm quickly on with what will turn out to be my only yellowtail.

From the bridge, Howell eyes my fluorocarbon leader disapprovingly. "Twelve-pound pink Ande mono will outfish fluoro here," he says. "See that guy?" A customer who has spooled up with the stuff is fast into his seventh fish. But I already have my yellowtail, so I can't focus on this terrific fishing for one of the most delicately flavored fish in the ocean, anyway. But I'm okay with that. I think.

Hill has me change rigs again, and I luck into a blue runner (No. 7). Yet another change gets me a smashing hit from a barracuda, but I can't stick the hooks. Still, I'm up to seven species.

Back on shore I grab lunch and return to Robbie's, where I paddle one of their kayaks out to a mangrove creek on the Gulf side of the key. I've been instructed to go past the second bend, tie off to a branch, drop a chum bag, and toss a lightly weighted live shrimp into the slick.

The creek is narrow and shady with a deceptively quick current, but I'm comfortable in this setup because I fish Barnegat Bay from a kayak back home in New Jersey. That's also why the feel of a fly landing on my inner thigh as I sit spread-eagled in the 'yak doesn't seem out of place. I am concentrating on the fishing and try to shake the fly off without taking my eyes from my line. When it doesn't move and I look down to see not a fly but a silver dollar–size crab disappearing up my shorts leg, I nearly capsize.

I quickly remove the crab, the creek eventually settles back down, and the orange-finned schoolmasters and gray (mangrove) snappers smack the shrimp. That brings my species count up to nine; my phantom-itch count in bed that night reaches about 3,000.

When I was 15 years old, I was fascinated by the book *A Journey to Matecumbe* by Robert Lewis Taylor. In it the young Davey Burnie travels by dugout canoe through the Everglades on his way to the Florida Keys, sleeping on island hummocks and eating stew made from alligators that were captured by Seminoles.

What backcountry guide Jim Willcox and I are looking at, however, is nothing so mundane as a gator. It is an American crocodile, a 12-footer resting in the dappled shade of the mangroves out here where the Everglades meet Florida Bay. This is one of about a thousand crocodiles that inhabit the southern tip of Florida, and Willcox has beached the bow of his 18-foot Action Craft flats boat on the island so we can get a better look at it.

American crocs are a threatened species, downgraded from the endangered list last year. Right now, though, I'm the species that feels unsafe. The croc is 30 feet away.

"That's a big one," says Willcox. "But even big ones are fast." I shift my weight from starboard to port to make sure that the hull isn't stuck fast in the marl.

We've motored about an hour from Bud N' Mary's Marina in Islamorada through Florida Bay to get to this maze of islands, shoals, broad expanses of water, and snakelike creeks. Willcox, 52, seems to know every inch of it.

The day before, Willcox and I had fished a number of patch reefs—isolated coral outcroppings within a mile or two of shore—and added eight species to the list. Willcox wanted to fish the backcountry today so I could reach my halfway point.

And we've done well. So far today I've caught sea catfish (No. 18), jack crevalle (No. 19), spotted seatrout (No. 21), snook (No. 22) and, in a model of fishing efficiency, a 100-pound bull shark (No. 23) that ate a ladyfish (No. 20). I also jumped and lost a tarpon, but my self-imposed IGFA tournament rules dictate that a fish isn't considered caught unless I bring it close enough for me to touch the leader.

What I need to catch is a redfish. But here, in the slow current of the creek bend, I am hooking snook after snook.

"Let's get the hell out of here," says Willcox. "The snook are biting like crazy." He looks at me. "I've never said that before in my life."

We motor through open water to a heavily shoaled shoreline. We have to anchor the boat and walk through shallows to get to the mouth of a tiny mangrove- and cypress-lined flowage that Willcox says is home to my redfish.

The outgoing tide is very warm, exposing shoals that are ankle-deep with seashells that would cost a dollar each at a Miami airport souvenir shop. Along the shoreline I see cuts and holes, channels and dropoffs, eddies and deadfalls. We haven't seen another fisherman in hours. I want to stay right here for the next four to six weeks and fish it all. But Willcox points to the creek. "Cast a shrimp upcurrent," he says. I slowly wade toward the mouth, working the waist-deep water as I go. On my fourth cast my line wraps around an overhanging mangrove branch, and I have to cross to the steep opposite bank to free it.

I swing the rod to loop the line off the branch, and that, of course, is when the redfish sucks in the shrimp.

The creek is about 10 feet wide, the red is about 6 pounds, and I can see about 300 places for him to wrap me. But I'm not going to lose this fish, which now wants to swim back through the Everglades and all the way to Lake Okeechobee. I hear Willcox rapidly sloshing through the water toward me. "Just beach it!" he's yelling.

I'd once lost a 5-pound smallmouth trying to do just that on a Pennsylvania lake when my landing net was lying forgotten somewhere, but I have no other option. I crank down on the fish and in one motion sweep the rod back, take two steps up, and drag the red onto the bank. Then I fall like a sack of cement so my body is between water and fish, and pin it with my forearm. Willcox gets there a few seconds later. "Smooth," he says. "You're not ready for AARP yet!"

By the time we get back to the dock, I've reached 27 species. More than halfway, and time to get out on the big water.

In *The Old Man and the Sea*, Ernest Hemingway's Santiago battles an 18-foot blue marlin from a skiff in the Florida Straits, where the Gulf Stream begins between Cuba and the Florida Keys. I am in those very waters now and much better equipped than Santiago, who had only a hook and a handline. I'm sitting in a fighting chair on the deck of the 56-foot Catch-22, piloted by Capt. Scott Stanczyk. I watch as mates Nick Stanczyk, Scott's nephew, and K.J. Zeher carefully put a rod with a Penn International 80 reel loaded with 100-pound-test line in the gimbal between my legs.

The reel's giant spool looks sparse at the moment, though, because at the other end of the quarter mile of line leading from the rod tip and practically straight down from the transom is, we hope, a big broadbill swordfish.

To get here we passed through the waters I was in yesterday with Adler on his Kalex, where I caught that little saddle bass (No. 43) we all argued about, and 19 other species. Some were truly incredible—from the impossibly tiny-mouthed filefish (No. 32), to the blue parrotfish (No. 35) that looked like wet sapphire, to the 2-foot-long remora (No. 34) that Adler insisted could adhere to my belly and hang there (it did, and the sensation was like having a vacuum-cleaner hose with a thousand tiny needles at its end stuck to your skin).

I ended the day by catching a behemoth 25-pound permit—my 47th species, and a trophy fish on any trip—and we whooped and hollered our way back to the marina.

Here on the Catch-22, though, everyone is quiet as the boat rises and falls in the swells, as if the big billfish more than 1,500 feet below could sense us. I knew that Richard Stanczyk—the owner of Bud N' Mary's, who is on board today, directing operations—had perfected a method of fishing for swordfish in daylight, involving 10 pounds of concrete weight, several large lightsticks, a large baitfish (today's was a butterflied 5-pound cero), and a hell of a lot of line. What I didn't know was that we would troll up a blackfin tuna and an almaco jack on the 40-mile ride out here, meaning I'd have a shot at a sword for my 50th species.

Nick is perched on the transom, the line from my rod in his gloved hand. "He's on," he says to me, almost casually.

"Huh?" I say stupidly.

"He's on! Start cranking!"

It takes me a few minutes to feel the fish but there's no doubt when I do. Zeher—who mates on a number of boats out of Bud N' Mary's—slips a fighting harness around me and clips the reel to it, so I can lean back to gain slack, then reel it in as I drop forward. Do this a couple of hundred times with a fish almost as big as you on the other end of the line, and you start wondering how much ibuprofen is on board.

I'm alternating between cranking, cursing, and praying as the fish turns and peels off a football field's length of my preciously gained line, then seems to have shaken the hook when the line goes slack. But he's still there. He's swimming toward the surface, and in a few minutes I see the electric gray of his flank. Nick and Zeher are ready with gaffs, and the 125-pound sword is eventually in the boat, thumping and thrashing. There is a lot of emotional yelling from everyone on board.

I've done it. But I realize something else.

Among all the backslaps and grins and handshakes, I know that these men and all the other guides on this trip are happy not just for my accomplishment but for their contribution to it. Like me, fishing makes them feel good about life. Besides, my 50-species one-week midlife slam became a personal challenge for them; a test of their fishing knowledge and prowess. Helping me attain that goal was a way of proving their ability.

"You did it!" says Nick.

"We sure did," I say.

My last day here is with Capt. Vic Gaspeny, a bonefish and tarpon fishing legend on these waters. My 16-year-old son, Joe, is with me, and he wants to catch his first bone. I've never caught one either, but after the largesse of the week and hitting my goal of 50, I'm content to watch.

Gaspeny anchors on a flat within shouting distance of U.S. 1 and casts out lightly weighted shrimp from four rods. One of them twitches less than 10 minutes later, and Joe is soon running miniature laps around the boat, trying to keep a straight line angle to the bone. Gaspeny eventually nets the 4-pounder.

Joe repeats the exercise a few minutes later, and again soon after that. He's caught 11 pounds of bonefish in about an hour, and when a rod twitches for the fourth time, I grab it. Joe and Gaspeny laugh. "Change your mind, Dad?" asks Joe.

"One for good luck," I say. The bone tears off, the spool spins, and I think, *I never caught a tarpon. Could I catch 60 tarpon in a week?*

FLYFISHING GONE MAD

KIRK DEETER

I was the bag man, there to stuff burlap sacks with body parts. We were in a dim alley behind a San Diego fish market. Conway Bowman's feet dangled over the edge of a Dumpster as he tossed tuna carcasses over the rim.

"Oh, bitchin'. Check these out," Bowman said as he slid to the ground and handed me two albacore bellies, the Dom Perignon of chum. We threw them in the sacks, nodded at two puzzled onlookers, and headed toward the Dana Landing Marina, where we would launch our chase for shortfin mako sharks on the fly.

Shortfin makos have been the focus of fishing lore for generations. They frequently occupied the tales of Ernest Hemingway and Zane Grey. But Bowman's angle pushes the edge of reason. It goes like this: Motor anywhere from 5 to 30 miles off the Southern California coast in a 24-foot open hull boat until the ocean floor drops away into canyons over a thousand feet deep. There, you ride the swells above schooling baitfish, mackerel, and tuna to chum, tease, and hook a predator as large as yourself on a 14-weight fly rod.

Imagine tying your fly line around the waist of NFL wide receiver Terrell Owens and hanging on as he runs a deep route. These sharks swim three

times faster than T.O. sprints—up to 60 mph—and could easily hurdle the goal's crossbar.

Several weeks earlier, Bowman and his protégé, Capt. Dave Trimble, had invited me and a couple of pals to spend a week fishing the new-moon tides. It would be the flyfishing equivalent of a Warren Miller extreme skiing movie—crashing on Bowman's floor, on the boats early, fishing hard all day, licking our wounds at night, and getting up to do it again. After some convincing, photographer Bill Decker agreed to tag along in a chase boat. The 58-year-old surfer and board fisherman was not fazed by the sharks; his reservations were about the flyfishing, "a sissy sport," as he liked to call it.

Once the team was assembled, we loaded the boats with our gear and chum stash and idled away from Mission Bay. I was nervous. You always feel anticipation as you head out on the water, but your worries are limited to *Will I make the casts*, *Did I apply enough sunscreen* or, at the worst, *I hope I don't puke*. On a mako trip, you worry that you might not come back whole. What sets these sharks apart from anything else you catch with a fly rod is that they can kill you. Before the trip, a friend had e-mailed me a story about a Delaware charter captain who died when his hand got tangled in a wire leader and the mako on the other end ripped him overboard like a rag doll.

Makos are apex predators, torpedo shaped and all muscle, with layered rows of razorlike teeth. Although they have not earned the notoriety of bull sharks or great whites because they typically cruise deeper offshore waters, makos can be just as nasty. They're vicious even before birth; they cannibalistically devour their weaker siblings in utero. They have also been known to attack boats, and if one jumps in the boat with you, it can unleash a world of hurt. As a rule of thumb, when a mako jumps in, you jump out and hope he doesn't have friends nearby.

The hull bounced hard on the water as we rode toward a GPS point named "Top of the Nine." We carried no guns, no gaffs, no means to subdue the mako. The best we could hope for was a draw. When the angler pulled the shark close to the boat, Bowman or Trimble would grab the leader and slide an improvised long-handled release tool into its mouth to pop the fly. Then you'd start over. For these guys, it was all a big game.

After half an hour, Bowman killed the motor and tied the burlap chum sacks to the side of the boat. We rigged wire leaders to gaudy red and orange flies. Thirteen miles offshore, I could barely see the silhouette of Point Loma. "Keep your eyes open," Bowman warned. Everything was hushed, save the steady breeze and swells lifting and slapping against the hull. "We have a good chance of seeing a big shark."

The truth is that "a big shark" out here is still young. The California Bight, where the ocean indents the coast off of San Diego, is one of three major mako breeding grounds in the world. (The other two are off New Zealand and Madagascar.) Recently pupped makos will hang around this area for two years before ranging out to sea.

It's a nursery, brimming with juvenile fish. The average mako cruising into a slick is about 80 pounds, but adults occasionally show up. A grown female can weigh over 1,300 pounds, and mature males can reach 500 pounds or more. Still, both captains say they rarely see sharks this size, and when they do, they don't cast at them—usually.

"There is a threshold for flyfishing, and sometimes you need to check your ego and just watch the fish swim by," Trimble said. "The pictures you see of huge makos caught off the east coast, that's a totally different business. They're caught with bait and balloons on heavy tackle. And fishermen kill the sharks to land them. Here, hooking, landing, and releasing a 150-pound mako on a fly rod is enough to kick your ass. And we can do that five or six times—which is like catching five or six tarpon—in a morning."

For the record, Bowman claims the biggest mako he has landed on the fly was in the 275- to 300-pound range. Trimble and a client once hooked and nearly landed a mako they figured to be around 500 pounds. I had set a lofty goal of catching one in the neighborhood of 200 pounds. As it turned out, I only had to wait about an hour for my opportunity.

Ever since Bowman had dropped the chum bags in the water, Jeremy Hyatt had been craning his neck over the side, waiting for action. Hyatt is classic Colorado—a trout guide, rock climber, and whitewater kayaker—and we had brought him and Colorado fly shop owner Dan Hydinger along to get a comparative thrill reading when the sharks showed up. Now, as the first fin cut the water, Hyatt was pointing and howling wildly.

There is no rhyme or reason for when and how makos appear. Sometimes, on the ride offshore in the early morning, when the seas are calm and the wind is light, you might see one cruising under flocks of birds, or around kelp patties. Once you've set up a chum line, it might take five minutes or two hours for one to show. Or it might not happen at all.

If you use a surf-casting rod to throw a mackerel-head teaser around the boat, out of nowhere, a mouth may pop up and grab it. But most often, the mako arrives on its own terms, when you aren't expecting it. You may be laughing, talking, or eating lunch. Then, as you lean over to fling away a pickle slice from your sandwich, a 6-footer glides by within an arm's reach.

It's like hunting big game from a tree stand. You go from a semihypnotic trance to sheer internal chaos in under two seconds. One instant, you're barely awake, and the next, your heart is in your throat. That's how it happened with this first mako.

"He's a gorilla. One-eighty, maybe 200," Bowman shouted as Hyatt and I scrambled around the deck. "I'm going to get him fired up." He dangled a mackerel head in front of the shark and ripped it away just before the shark lunged, banged the boat, and then circled out into the slick. Bowman dragged the teaser through the chum line again, like a bullfighter with a cape, then once more, from another direction. With each pass, the fish got more pissed off.

I threw a fly into the mayhem and gave the line a sharp tug to pull it taut. The shark spun an angry arc looking for the teaser but found my fly instead. He bit down and swam toward the boat. Not wanting to set the hook while the mako was headed in my direction, I gave him slack line as he spit the fly. No problem. Sharks are used to eating things that poke them in the mouth. Within a minute, he was back.

Another cast, another strip, another bite. This time he turned away from the boat, and I set the hook with three hard jerks. In seconds the shark had unspooled the fly line, then ripped backing off the reel so fast that the powder residue on the gel-spun material looked like yellow smoke piping through the line guides. As I braced the rod butt into my thigh, I accidentally bumped my hand against the whirring reel. It cut my right thumb as if I had brushed against a band saw.

The shark jumped twice, cartwheeling over the waves. Then, for 30 minutes, I cranked the rod down toward the surface, strained and lifted, then cranked again, gaining sacred inches of line and occasionally licking the blood off my thumb. Eventually, we cheated and motored up on the fish to gather 200-plus yards of backing and fly line. Decker, shouting from the chase boat, said he wanted photos. I wanted this battle to end, one way or the other. When we were finally close enough for Bowman to grab the wire, the mako thrashed his head, snapped at Bowman's arm, and stretched his jaws so wide we could have dropped a 5-gallon bucket inside his mouth.

"That fish was 200," Bowman said as the shark finned away and we wiped the sweat off our faces. I flexed my left hand open and shut to coax blood flow back into my forearm. I was toast.

We spent the next several days working the same drill—Hyatt, Hydinger, and I trading turns hooking and fighting makos, and Decker firing away with the shutter, barking "Get closer!" as sharks leaped around the boats. After a while, we even got a bit comfortable with the routine. But that didn't last.

One night, late in the week, we found ourselves rolling through La Jolla in Trimble's classic ragtop Cadillac Eldorado. He drove with the seat half reclined, his left arm resting on top of the steering wheel. At that angle, I got a good look at the detailed tattoo of a mako chasing yellowfins on his forearm.

"Is Decker serious about the kayak?" he asked Bowman.

"Yeah, he says he wants to get pictures of us fighting a mako from one," Bowman said. I figured they were joking.

Sure enough, at 6:30 the next morning, Decker sauntered down the dock with a blue sea kayak balanced on his head. Two hours later, we were back on "Top of the Nine," bobbing in silence, when the first mako, maybe an 80-pounder, came barreling up the oily slick.

We traded glances as Decker dropped the kayak in the water. For a long moment, there were no volunteers. Then Bowman handed Hydinger the teaser rod, picked up the paddle and a fly rod, and jumped in. I was running the chase boat, feeling as if I was about to watch a train wreck.

The shark was hot even before Hydinger started throwing the teaser. At one point it circled toward the mackerel head and bumped against the kayak. It's difficult enough to cast an oversize fly when you are upright, let alone when you're sitting on a wobbly hunk of plastic with a paddle on your lap. Bowman managed one short cast with a popper fly, which prompted the mako to spin and look but not bite. Swells pushed the kayak farther away from the slick, and the shark disappeared.

As Bowman paddled back into the slick to set up for another cast, Hydinger called out, "Here's another shark!"

"It's not the same one?" Bowman asked.

"Nope. This one's twice as big." As the fin skimmed past Bowman, we saw this shark was longer than the kayak. I was about to suggest we call this deal off when Bowman cast and began popping the fly across the surface. Pop. Pop. Chomp. The mako swirled at a right angle, pulling the kayak sideways against the swells. Bowman teetered, then leaned to steer the craft in line with the rod, which was banging against the hull as the shark tore line off the screaming reel.

The drag was tight enough that the mako began to tow the kayak. We marked a waypoint on the GPS and ran the motors to catch up. We wanted to be close enough to grab Bowman if something went wrong, though most of us realized that if he fell out, he would likely be in greater trouble than we could save him from. As we watched Bowman strain against the shark, plowing a dogged path through the waves, this kayak idea felt like a joke gone very wrong.

The shark dragged the boat for nearly a half mile before Bowman started gaining line, bowing over the front of the kayak, then leaning on his back as he worked the reel. He cranked in all the backing, then started up the fly line through the running line into the belly. But what was he going to do next?

"If that shark does something weird, drop the rod, and forget about it," Decker yelled.

"We'll reach over and pull you in the boat. You can land the fish from here," I shouted.

And then suddenly, the line went slack. The shark was gone. We motored over and hauled Bowman and the kayak into our boat. He showed us the line. It had been sawed through, just above the leader. Maybe the shark had cut it with his tail. Maybe he had bitten through it after turning back on Bowman. We'll never know.

That night over mai tais at the dockside bar, we talked about the last few days. Bowman grinned and shook his head. "That kayak was a little dicey," he said. "I don't think I'll be doing that again soon. It sets a bad example for the kids." We made plans to fish together again later in the year, but on my water instead, in a trout stream in Colorado. I promised him we'd go extreme in the high country. Heck, we could hike above the treeline. It might even snow.

MUCHA TRUCHA GRANDE!

JONATHAN MILES

With the notable exceptions of rum drinks, black beans, fat brown cigars, the smiles of pretty girls, hot yellow sunlight, and fat men with guitars and bongos playing mambos, rumbas, and boleros late into the night, nothing in Cuba comes easily. Take, for example, bass fishing. For the smattering of bass anglers living in Cuba, the main obstacle is obtaining tackle. The 43-year-old U.S. trade embargo and Cuba's sputtering economy make bass lures hard to come by, forcing the more resourceful fishermen to manufacture their own artificial worms by dissolving old plastic shoe soles in mosquito repellent, over a flame, and then pouring the liquid into homemade 10-inch molds. Outboard motors are also rare: When the starter gun fires at a Cuban bass tournament, the anglers fan out in rowboats, thrashing the water as they paddle like hell to be first to the sweet spots.

For American bass anglers, the main obstacle is U.S. law, which effectively prohibits travel to Cuba. If you can get past that, however, there are the connect-the-dots travails of access. To fish one of Cuba's best bass lakes, for instance, requires a many-legged flight that includes a layover in a third country; then a 12-hour drive across the island on a two-lane highway hemmed with horse-drawn wagons, loping dogs, bicyclists, hitchhikers, and broken-down Russian minisedans; then a grueling, spine-compressing, two-hour drive on a pitted rural pathway bisecting sugarcane fields; and finally, at water's edge, a formal transaction with the lake's governmental boatmen, who inspect your passport and count your cash and stamp some papers and then stamp some other papers inside a dirt-floored wooden cabin where a bass calendar hangs upon the wall across from a neatly stacked shelf of empty Cristal beer cans.

The obvious question, then, is: Why? Why melt your precious shoes down to worms? Why flirt with—or even flaunt—the U.S. Treasury Department's ominously titled Trading With the Enemy Act? Why fly and then fly some more and then drive and drive some more, forfeiting your rental car deposit as you hammer the car's undercarriage into road rut after road rut? Why stand there in the tropical dawn trying to figure out how to get said rental car unstuck from its perch atop some railroad tracks? Why this just-shy-of-epic quest for a fish that about 90 miles to the north is so readily and conveniently available in almost every Florida park, pond, and puddle?

There is a very good and logical answer: Angling rumor has long held, over these many years of intransigent political standoff, that Cuba may harbor some of the best big-bass fishing in the world—with a fair claim to the next world-record largemouth.

Havana is one of the great cities of the world, sublimely tawdry yet stubbornly graceful, like tarnished chrome—a city, as a young Winston Churchill once wrote, where "anything might happen." Or at least this was what I told my pal Bruce Browning upon our arrival there, just before informing him that, because there are no bass in Havana, we would be leaving within the hour. As a journalist, I'd been to Cuba twice before, and though I'd circled every mention of bass fishing in my guidebooks, I'd never been able to fish there. But I'd talked about it a lot, mostly with Bruce, a professional bongo and conga drummer from Mississippi who shares my fascination with overweight fish. Cuba or bust, we pledged one night. Now we were making good on it.

In Havana, our party doubled: Dusan Smetana, a photographer, joined us, along with Samuel Yera—a three-time Cuban bass-tourney champion and perhaps the best bass angler in Cuba—who'd offered to guide us on our

cross-island bass odyssey. We piled our rods and tackle bags into a rented Toyota Yaris, a roundish microcar that would be ideal for parading Shriners but that shouldn't be marketed to traveling bass fishermen. As we motored out of Havana our kneecaps bumped our chins. The boys in the backseat swung their heads on the bumps to avoid getting eye-gouged by the rods rattling loosely between them. It was a decidedly Marxist (Harpo, not Karl) start to our trip.

We were going east toward Lake Hanabanilla, a deep, 7,900-acre impoundment in the Sierra Escambray mountains. "This," Samuel told me, "is the best lake in Cuba for the big bass. Last year, an Italian tourist caught a 17-pounder on a worm there, and back in the '80s, an American caught a 20- or 21-pounder. An uncertified catch, though." A former civil engineer, Samuel is soft-spoken and fine-featured, with the bearing and appearance of a campus intellectual, and while he's a keen conversationalist on a broad array of topics, one subject swims constantly through his brain: bass, or as it's called in Cuba, *trucha* (which in a vagary of language means "trout" to most Spanish speakers). More formally, it's known as *Lobina negra boquigrande*. In this case, the obsession is inherited. Samuel's father, Jose Manuel Yera, was the national bass champion in 1971 and '72, and Samuel's earliest memory is an image of rods and reels and worms and glittery lures. "For me," he said on the drive, as the Cuban countryside passed by in the dark, "it was a sickness for life." I told him that Bruce and I knew something about the sickness, and Dusan nodded knowingly. We were like a rolling support group.

Tucked into the high, pine-carpeted slopes of the Sierra Escambray, where it's cool even at noon and where the early-morning mist leaves a teardrop on every last green leaf and needle, Hanabanilla suggests lake trout more than bass—it almost seems too pretty for largemouths. Our quartet spent most of the next morning admiring it, waiting on two Triton bass boats with 75-horsepower Tracker engines that the Cuban government's tourism bureau recently purchased for the lake.

When the boats finally arrived, four hours late, we went at the lake hard, plugging at the shore structure with dark 10-inch worms and spinnerbaits, then trolling the old river channel with deep-diving crankbaits. The cobalt water here is startlingly clear, and with an average depth of 100 feet, it's unusually deep for a Cuban lake. A few scattered and smallish afternoon catches kept fish-despair at bay, but the action was slow. The fishfinder showed the bass suspended down in those depths, hanging low and motionless in the water.

Despite the un-basslike scenery, I trusted Samuel's testimony about more typical fishing days at Hanabanilla. Still, I couldn't help wondering: Was I the victim of dusty old hype? Was Cuba really the forbidden mecca of bass fishing, or was it, like areas in Mexico, just a patchwork of boom-and-bust lakes about which the breathless rumors always lag a few years (or decades) behind the reality?

These questions weighed darkly on my mind until close to midnight, when wandering the nearby Spanish colonial town of Trinidad, the four of us turned a corner at the Catedral Santísima Trinidad and found a street fair in raucous full swing, a salsa band sending drumbeats ricocheting around the plaza as dusky girls in wild headdresses danced on the cobblestones and teams of curbside bartenders muddled mint leaves for mojitos. After that, nothing weighed on my mind.

Until the following morning, that is. That's when I had to drive the little clown car nine hours across Cuba's eastern half. At one point we pulled alongside an oxbow to see what some anglers in float tubes were catching. I was hoping to see the freshwater eels that many Cuban handliners use for bait, and that may or may not be responsible for bass catches in excess of the official world record. (This is one of the juiciest rumors you hear about Cuba, that several or even many 22-pound-plus bass have been caught here—almost all of them by subsistence-fishing handliners throwing 1½-foot eels. Samuel said these catches were probable but that he'd never seen one, and that, for the record, the official Cuban mark was 18 pounds.) The float-tubers were local tilapia anglers, however, bobber-fishing with scrawny nightcrawlers, and they seemed quite uninterested in either catching or conversing about bass.

As we talked, a barefooted 5-year-old girl appeared from a shack atop a nearby hill and began lobbing chunks of driftwood into the water. This looked fun, so I joined her. When the girl's father came down to investigate, I explained that we were fishermen on our way to Lake Leonero, in Granma province, to try to catch *trucha*. His eyes widened. "*¿Lago Leonero?*" he asked with an envious grin. "*¡Mucha trucha grande!*" Opening his arms to demonstrate the size of the many *trucha grande* he was talking about, he looked like a man about to hug a 1,000-year-old tree. I sprinted so fervently back to the car that several cattle, including a bull, hustled out of my path. Bruce ran, too, but only because he doesn't speak Spanish and assumed I'd been threatened.

Unlike Hanabanilla, Leonero looks like a bass lake. In fact, Leonero looks like the perfect bass lake, the one you would design if you were God and needed to answer a pious fisherman's bedtime prayers. Long and shallow with coffee-colored water, dappled with lily pads and hemmed by 9-foot walls of cattails and bulrushes, Leonero sits in the middle of a vast and hard-to-access wetland in eastern Cuba, two difficult driving hours south of the nearest city of Bayamo. Leonero also lacks even the scantiest of amenities—there are no waterfront hotels here, nor lakeside restaurants where strolling string bands play "Guantanamera" and Eagles covers at your table. If you want to sleep at Leonero, you can wrestle a goat for a soft grassy knoll. If you want lunch, you bring it or catch it. And if you want to catch it, you park yourself in a creaky 14-foot wooden dinghy and let one of the lake's lackadaisical boatmen paddle and pole you slowly through the broken jigsaw puzzle of weeds and water.

We set out sometime after nine, focusing first on some narrow openings in the lily pad cover, pulling 10-inch pumpkinseed worms tenderly through the pad stems. It didn't take long for those stems to cough up *trucha*. "Big fish," Samuel whispered, leaning over the gunwales as he waited for the bass to swallow the worm, twitching the line ever so subtly. I'd never seen a bass fisherman with such artistic form and studied patience. He seemed more Zenned-out bonefisherman than hyperexcitable, rod-heaving basser—until he set the hook, that is, which is when I realized that the behavior of a man with a hooked bass completely transcends personality and geography. Samuel hollered and grinned and cussed as he fought the fish, his rod bending into a good solid U as he pried the bass from the weeds, and I swear that when he said, "C'mon, c'mon," he was speaking with an accent straight out of Eufaula, Alabama. "Nice fish," we said in unison, when he'd pulled it to the boat, because it was: 7 pounds 11 ounces, a hefty green football of a largemouth. The next bass was over 6 pounds, which set an unfortunate precedent—the 3- and 4-pounders we kept catching throughout the day felt like unqualified interlopers.

This is not to suggest that Leonero, where we fished for two days, was ever predictable. Patrolling the edges of the bulrushes yielded some of the bravura fishing you'd expect, but the open water was just as productive; at times, casting anywhere seemed as good as casting somewhere. Worms worked best in the mornings, and hard jerkbaits ruled the afternoons, but the deciding factor was always the lure's size—the bigger the lure, the better the fishing. I should clarify, though, that the old saw about small baits catching small fish and big baits catching big fish didn't apply here. Big baits caught fish. Small baits caught squat. An American angler from anywhere other than Texas, Florida, or California might feel a twinge of arrogance when tying on a bratwurst-size lure but that quickly subsides.

After two consecutive strikes right at the boat, and after scanning the flat expanse of water and registering no living creature save some peregrine falcons, scissorbill gulls, and savanna hawks, I asked the boatman how many bass anglers he'd taken out on the lake.

"Last year, eight," he said. He thought for a while, then added, "The year before, three."

Back in Havana, we huddled midday at the Bodeguita del Medio, a venerable saloon in the city's old quarter where decades' worth of signatures and rum-fueled graffiti cover the walls. We were drinking mojitos and talking about fish. More specifically, we were trying to pinpoint the giddy appeal of bass fishing in Cuba. True, we hadn't caught any glaring trophies—nothing above 10 pounds, though I did hook a cinder block of a bass at Leonero that, lunging sideways in open water, snapped the 17-pound-test connecting us. Nor had we pulled in the numbers of bass that make for tongue-wagging brochure copy; I'm certain we never hit triple digits either day at Leonero. But this line of thinking, we decided, is knuckleheaded at best. Fishing can be qualified but not quantified, especially in Cuba, where almost nothing can be quantified.

How, then, to describe bass fishing in Cuba? Maybe like this: In a corner of the Bodeguita del Medio, with the street outside awash in sunlight, an old man with a guitar and an old woman shaking maracas launched into a set of old Cuban folk songs, drowning out our earnest fish-talk. After a while, the old man passed out percussion instruments—more maracas, sticks known as claves, and a dried, hollow gourd—to us, and also to some Spanish girls who'd been languidly dancing and singing along with the musicians. I'm not sure what songs we all played that afternoon, but I can hear them as I type this. And when I close my eyes, visions of the guitar strings thrumming meld into visions of taut monofilament, images of the Spanish girls dancing meld into images of bass leaping on Leonero, seeming to uncoil atop the water, and I am brought to a place in my memory to which I yearn constantly to return: sunset at Leonero, with the croaks of bullfrogs and the whir of long casts keeping a slow, moody rhythm, the splash of topwater strikes like the steady crash of cymbals, with the coming Cuban night offering only more music, and the next day more fish.

COMPANY

LILYFISH

BILL HEAVEY

After the world takes an eggbeater to your soul, you never know what's going to get you up and back among the living. In my case, it was the ham. It was 3:30 on a sweltering July afternoon, three weeks to the hour since my new baby daughter lay down for a nap and woke up on the other side of this life.

I decided it was time to go fishing. There were any number of good reasons. For one, I could still smell Lily's baby sweetness in the corners of the house, still feel her small heft in the hollow of my shoulder. For another, I'd hardly left the house since she died and had taken to working my way through an alarming amount of dark rum and tonic each night, not a sustainable grief management technique over the long haul. Jane and I had planted the memorial pink crepe myrtle and the yellow lilies, chosen for having the audacity to bloom in the heat of the summer, the very time Lily died.

But it was the ham that got me off the dime. After the funeral, the neighbors had started bringing over hogs' hind legs as if the baby might rise from the dead and stop by for a sandwich if they could just get enough cured pork in the refrigerator. I knew my mind wasn't quite right, knew I still hadn't even accepted her death. But it seemed like I'd lose it unless I put some distance between me and the ham.

I shoved a small box of lures in a fanny pack, spooled up a spinning rod with 6-pound mono line, and filled a quart bottle with tap water. On my way out the door, I stopped, as I have taken to doing since her death, to touch the tiny blue urn on the mantel. "Baby girl," I said. I stood there for several minutes, feeling the coolness of fired clay and waiting for my eyes to clear again. Then I got in the car and drove 20 miles north of D.C. to the Seneca Breaks on the upper Potomac River.

I didn't particularly care that it was 102 degrees outside. I didn't particularly care that any smallmouth bass not yet parboiled by the worst heat wave in memory would scarcely be biting. I was furious at the world and everything still living in it now that my daughter wasn't. As I drove, the radio reported severe thunderstorms to the west and said they might be moving our way. Fine by me. If someone up there wanted to send a little electroshock therapy my way, I'd be easy to find.

Even at five o'clock the sun still had its noon fury. The heat had emptied the normally crowded parking lot at the river's edge. I stepped out of the air-conditioned car into the afternoon's slow oven. I slugged down some water, put my long-billed cap on, found a wading stick in the underbrush, and walked into the river. The water was bathtub warm and two feet below normal. Seneca Breaks, normally a mile-long series of fishy-looking riffles and rock gardens was, like the only angler fool enough to be out there, a ghost of its former self. At least it didn't smell like ham. But the fish weren't here, and I realized I shouldn't be either. It dawned on me that I'd better get in water that went over my waist or risk heatstroke.

Just upstream from the breaks, the river is called Seneca Lake, 3 miles of deep flats covered with mats of floating grass. I worked my way to the head of the breaks and slipped into this deeper water, casting a 4-inch plastic worm on a light sinker. Soon I'd waded out chin-deep into the lake, holding my rod arm just high enough to keep the reel out of the water. There were baitfish dimpling the surface every so often and dragonflies landing on my wrist, and once a small brown water snake wriggled by so close I could have touched him.

Nothing was hitting my worm, but that was to be expected. My arms

seemed to be working the rod on their own, and I was content to let them. I stood heron-still and felt the slow current brush grass against my legs. Every so often, a minnow would pucker up and take a little nip at my exposed leg. It tickled. Baby fish. I remembered how I'd call her Lilyfish sometimes when changing her diaper, remembered how she had loved to be naked and squiggling on the changing table, gazing up at me and gurgling with something approaching rapture as I pulled at her arms and legs to stretch them.

The tears welled up again. I found the melody to an old Pete Townshend song running circles through my head and finally latched onto the chorus:

After the fire, the fire still burns,
The heart grows older but never ever learns.

That's how it was, alright. The fire was gone, but it still burned. It would always burn. The memories—her smell, her smile, the weight of her in my arms—would always smolder. And I'd always yearn for the one thing I'd never have.

And what struck me as I stood alone in the middle of the river was that while my world had been changed forever, the world itself had not changed a whit. The river simply went about its business. A dead catfish, bloated and colorless, washed serenely past, on its way back down the food chain. The sun hammered down, and a hot wind wandered the water.

I caught a bluegill, then two little smallmouths, within 10 minutes of each other. As I brought the fish to the surface, I had the sensation of bringing creatures from a parallel universe into my own for a minute before sending them darting back home. I wondered if death might be like this, traveling to a place where you didn't think it was possible to breathe, only to arrive discovering that you could. I hoped it was. The older I get, the more I believe that there is such a thing as the soul, that energy changes form but still retains something it never loses. I hoped that Lily's soul was safe. That she knew how much she was still loved.

I don't know how long i stayed there or even if I kept fishing. I remember looking up at some point and noticing that the light had softened. It was after eight and the sun was finally headed into the trees. And now, just like every summer night for eons, the birds came out: an osprey flying recon over the shallows 50 feet up; a great blue heron flapping deep and slow, straight toward me out of the fireball, settling atop a rock and locking into hunting stance. And everywhere swallows coming out like twinkling spirits to test who could trace the most intricate patterns in the air, trailing their liquid songs behind them.

Suddenly I wasn't angry anymore. This is the world, I realized for the millionth time, and its unfathomable mystery: always and never the same, composed in roughly equal parts of suffering and wonder, unmoved by either, endlessly rolling away. It was getting dark now, hard to see the stones beneath the water. I waded carefully back to my car, rested the stick by a post for another fisherman to use, changed into dry clothes, and drove home.

Take your grief one day at a time, someone had told me. I hadn't known what he meant at the time, but I did now. This had been a good day. Lily, you are always in my heart.

FISHING WITH DAD

KEITH MCCAFFERTY

My father was a night fisherman, a quiet, self-reliant man who wore old felt fedoras and smoked a pipe to keep the bugs at bay. He lit our campfire with matches struck on his thumbnail, then picked up his fly rod and walked into the sunset alone.

Once or twice during the summer, when our family put up a tent on Michigan's Platte River, he would pile us all into the car to go to the Cherry Bowl Drive-In Theater. There we would watch the double feature while Dad hiked down the hill into a birch bottom along the river. When he returned during the second bill, my little brother and I would clamber out of the car to look at the gleaming sides of the trout against his waders. It could be Gary Cooper on the screen, 30 feet tall with a Colt on his hip, but in those moments it was Dad who was the star.

On the night I became his disciple, there had been no hint beyond a whispered argument with my mother that he would permit me to accompany him. Until then, I had never followed any farther than the bank before returning to the security of the fire, where my brother and I would roast marshmallows while Mom sat with a book and a Siamese cat on her lap. This night—I was 7 or 8 years old and we were camped on the Au Sable River—Dad said not one word to me. But after pulling on his waders he helped me into mine, cinched an Army belt around my waist, and revolved a spray can of 6-12 mosquito repellent around my head. I endured this with my face screwed up under the stinging mist, and then we walked away from the tent where my mother stood with lines of concern on her face, as if she were watching us board a train leaving for war. We hiked down a twisted path into the cedar swamp, the light from the camp lanterns growing faint behind us. My waders accordioned down my legs and made a squeaking sound. The song of the river came and went and rose again more insistently.

I looked up at Dad as he tamped tobacco into his pipe. Above us, a black rope of mayflies stitched the slot of sky between the cedars. As the river lost its polish, the flies flew lower and lower until, one by one, they dropped to the surface, their wings spread like crucifixes. A trout rose, then another, the first drops of a coming rain. Then an abrupt, deep wallop interrupted the patter.

"You hear him? There, down under the sweeper. That's a good feesh."

Dad was the great-grandson of Irish immigrants who had settled in the Appalachians to mine coal, and his speech carried mountain inflections—a cushion was a "cooshion," a fish was a "feesh."

The bowl of Dad's pipe made a cherry circle. It glowed farther and farther downstream as he worked into position. I heard the whistle of the fly line and then a ruckus on the surface. It drew me out of my fear, for without his hand to hold I had been afraid to take a step. Tentatively, I stubbed my toes around the submerged logs and came up beside him.

"Hold on to the rod," he said.

The weight unbent my arm. I had it only a minute before Dad put his hand over mine. Then he took the rod and netted the trout, and together we looked down at it, heavy and silver-sided in the light of his headlamp. Back at camp, he laid it on a punky log and opened his knife. Dad slit the fish's belly and pumped a mass of undigested mayflies from its stomach. I carried it back to the tent, with four fingers hooked inside its gills, and its sweet, coppery smell was still on my hands in the morning.

FISHING WITH DAD

This, then, would be the legacy he passed on to me: the smells, the sights, the sounds of night. The treasure of trout. Magic of rivers.

My father grew up in the Depression, drove trains for the 759th Railway Operating Battalion in World War II, and would work 35 years as a locomotive engineer for the Pennsylvania Railroad. A taciturn man, he never mastered the social graces that might have allowed us to be friends in an easy way. But the sense of isolation he carried around in everyday living wore better at the river. His voice, gruff with frustration, grew soft when water was near. It was as if the river smoothed him in the manner that it sands rough rock into polished stone. I believe that when he handed me the rod, he was parting with as much of himself as he knew how to, in a language that didn't require a facility with words.

After that night on the Au Sable I became his shadow, the son who traipsed two paces behind, tripping on roots as we hiked one black path after another along the Indian rivers of the Upper and Lower Peninsulas: the Two Hearted and the Little Manistee, the Pigeon, the Muskegon, and the Tittabawassee. Dad taught me to tie flies, and soon I graduated beyond the rudimentary skills of his blunt fingers. I came to tie not only for him but also, by the time I was 10, for entire campgrounds of trout fishermen. As my legs grew, I became the one to lead the way to the river as often as not. A night came when who was holding whose hand across the deep part changed, and that marked an end of hero worship and the beginning of something far more complex.

No longer in his shadow, I grew somewhat estranged from Dad, a situation that had to do with the times and my age—a common enough story of fathers who turned inward after the war and sons who grew into their teens during the 1960s. I began to see his frailties as well as his strengths. Tragedies that had claimed both his father and his mother had left scars that would never disappear. He was a perfectionist but an imperfect man, and sometimes it seemed like I could never do anything right. It was left to the rivers to exert their magic, pulling us as if by colorless ropes to banks of common ground, where for a few weeks every summer we lived as all fathers and sons should live. On a river, the gulf between us seemed less pronounced than it was at home. A difference of opinion could be forgotten there, a hard word forgiven. Silence was absorbed by the sound of the current. No other place ever afforded us such sanctuary.

The next bend in our relationship took place on water, though it was not on the banks of a river. I had finished college and was working my way around the country before graduate school. My first job was selling fishing tackle in Islamorada in the Florida Keys, and when Dad came to visit, I took him fishing. It had always been his dream to catch a bonefish, but like so many others, this one had been submerged under the day-to-day of life, passed to the next generation to become reality.

We waded onto the flat in the evening, spooking midget barracudas that shot over the turtle grass. I tried to impress on Dad the necessity of casting quickly for distance. While he practiced the tide went out, and when it came back the light was going and out there, way out there like the dream that had been beyond his reach, bonefish started to tail. My father waved his rod expansively. His casts fell miserably short of the mark. I only talked the talk—my own casting collapsed immediately. The bonefish wagged their tails like fingers. The evening fell to its polished, pewter curtain, magnifying our mistakes. Then I cast beyond my reach, a gift that put the fly on the nose of a bonefish tilted down, its wondrous liquid tail wagging, wagging, wagging.

I had him.

"Look," I said to Dad as the fish veered off on a tangent. A transparent sheet of water jumped up the line. The fish was far into the backing before it stopped.

I did not know I was going to hand my father the rod until I did.

"Here, keep the tip high," I told him. "Isn't he strong?"

"He's strong all right, Kam," he said.

Then the line stopped moving and Dad started to reel.

"I can't feel him."

My fists jumped for the rod. I stripped line frantically until at last it snapped taut. "No, he just ran toward us," I said, and from that point Dad fought the fish, its runs growing shorter until it was turning arcs 40 feet out.

"You better land him, Kam," he said. "I don't want you to lose him."

FISHING WITH DAD

When I put on the pressure, it swam right in. Cradling a hand under the bonefish, I lifted. Little more than a dozen years after I had become mesmerized staring at the trout my father caught and netted for me on the Au Sable, our roles had reversed. Dad gazed at the bonefish with his head tilted to the side, leaning back to bring it into focus, as he had left his glasses back in the car. He looked from the fish to me and back again.

I think it was at that moment that something inside him relaxed. The edge of tension between us eased. In a sense, I emerged as the fisherman for both of us.

After that trip to the Keys, Dad began a slow fade from the water. In his fifties by then, he had already suffered the first of a string of heart attacks that left him with poor circulation, so that his work-hardened hands felt cold to the touch. He couldn't get his fingers to flex and might spend half an hour struggling into his waders while I caught trout.

I understood this incompletely. One fall, when he joined me on a camping trip in Yellowstone Park, it baffled me that he wouldn't get out of his sleeping bag early enough to fish the Madison River. No matter that it was 12 degrees, the stars just losing their edges; if you could get a marabou deep in the current, those big browns jumped all over it. Didn't he see there were fish down there?

Eventually he left the river for long periods in favor of practice casting on his lawn. This happened after he had retired to Montana, where I also had moved to start a family. Three trout streams passed within a few miles of Dad's front door. He paid them no attention. The backyard was his river now; his cat, pouncing on the line, was a fickle trout. This pantomime respected no season. Opening day came and went according to his state of mind. The fly line rolled over grass and snow. The guides on the rod wore out. And the cat grew noticeably older. Dad kept right on casting.

It's been suggested that there are four stages in a fisherman's life—from wanting to catch any fish to many fish, from wanting to catch many fish to the biggest fish, and finally to being satisfied only by the most challenging fish. Dad had arrived on higher ground. He didn't need the fish—or even the river.

That his casting was a calming influence I could grasp. The old man had always been a champion fidgeter. Once, while standing in line to use the bathroom in the first grade, he had fidgeted so badly with the matches in his pocket that he set his pants on fire—he'd been bringing cigarettes to school since he was 5 years old.

Now, entering his seventies, his hands began to quiver not so much from nerves as from the insidious advance of Parkinson's disease. When I lightheartedly asked him why he didn't fish, he said seriously, "Kam, I can't tie the fly on anymore."

After that, I rigged up flies tied onto tippets so that he could loop them to the end of his leader. It helped, but his eventual return to the river had less to do with me than with the generation in the wings. When my son, Tom, became old enough to take his turn as a fisherman's shadow, it was my father's boots that he followed. Dad had someone new to teach, to take by the hand into the river's darkness.

Who says there are no second acts in an angler's life? He became a fine fisherman on our local rivers and a familiar figure with his Greek fisherman's cap and salt-and-pepper mustache, his fly line dancing over the blue riffles. He was a mentor to many young anglers who benefited from his generosity and wisdom. If I have a regret about this time in our relationship, it is that I seldom went with him. My days on the water were reserved for longer rods, deeper currents, and bigger fish—I was still bent to a stretch of road where pounds mattered. It was through raising my own son that I came to realize what I was missing, and after that I would steal an hour or two each week to fish with Dad, usually at night. During those times, in the darkness that laid bare our dependence on each other, I came to understand that we were together on one path after all, even if many years and many miles apart.

In his last decade, Dad lived on the Missouri River where he and my mother had built a house. Unsteady on his feet, he used a ski pole for balance and seldom managed a cast of more than 20 feet. He fished with wind knots in his leader, and it was probably a knot that cost him the biggest trout he'd ever hooked. It rose to a caddis imitation one July; he had it on only a few seconds before the leader broke. A week later he hooked it again and fought it for half an hour by the watch, with my mother trailing behind him through the weeds in her open-toed sandals, carrying a pike net, Dad's old dog Max bringing up the rear. I wish I could say he landed it, but he was the kind of man who never stretched a fish, let alone claimed one that parted his company.

"Kam," he said when I saw him next, "that was a mighty big feesh." He shook his head, his eyes bright and clear so that, for just a second, you could see the boy in him. You could see yourself in him. You could see your son.

This was the father I remembered when my brother and I scattered his ashes over the Missouri River last Christmas Eve. The act was cathartic, for he had died less than a month before and I had become haunted by my last vision of him, gasping for breath in a hospital bed as I read aloud stories that I had written. It was hard to believe that this broken man was the same one who had played such a large role in those stories. But the ashes seemed to spirit the ghost of his final days away with the breeze, and when the memorial service ended, I walked back down the bank with a lighter step than I'd had in a long time.

We had donned waders to scatter the ashes, and I stepped into the shallows among the white pepper of his bone chips with a fly rod in my hand. It was not really a fish I was after so much as my father's presence, for it had been here, on a spring day nearly a year before, that he and I spent our last hour together on a river. On that afternoon, I'd held his hand to help him wade out to the gravel bar. While he stood uncertainly with his ears turning red—March can be cold in Montana—I waltzed a streamer fly through the riffle until I caught a trout.

"Here," I told him, "you take the rod."

The hand he extended shook so badly that I had to place my own upon it, settling it while the trout fought.

"That's a good feesh, Kam," he said when the fish swam into view. He bent over with his nose dripping while I worked the hook free, and then the trout, the last he would ever touch with a rod, wavered for a moment over sunlit pebbles before vanishing into the depths.

Now, I once again was able to feel his hand against mine as I cast. But it was no longer the hand of winter's memory, liver-spotted and made cold by disease; this was a warm hand unmarked by age, guiding mine. It was the wrong time of year to expect much cooperation from the trout, but I was not surprised when the fly stopped in the current below me. The fish was a fine brown, big-spotted like the midnight trout from the Au Sable. It seemed a fitting Christmas gift from the man who had guided me on the path to the river, and as I bent down to slip the hook, I was able to see in my own reflection the father who had held my hand where the river ran deep.

GRATITUDE

DAVE HURTEAU

The day my grandfather died he said he was going fishing, but he only made it as far as the bathroom. It was the best he could do.

I was supposed to go out with him. "C'mon, Friend!"

That's what he called me. Like this: "Friend! Get me a beer!" and "Friend! Come hill my potatoes!" He also called me "No Friend." Like this: "No Friend! What'sa matter with you? You got a screw loose?"

Anyway, I knew he wouldn't make it. But I suspected he wanted once more to drive his putt-putting red Omni to the Dyke Road—a gravel lane where he'd lately been pulling to a stop in the middle of the road above the culvert, opening the car door, and casting from the driver's seat into the pool below.

It was, like I said, the best he could do.

A few years earlier, before his legs would no longer carry him to the stream bank; before the hit-and-run incident in which he gunned the big Chrysler he drove then out of his driveway in reverse, creamed my brother's parked new car, shifted into drive and went fishing; before it was decided that he could no longer be trusted with a car that topped 40 mph, I did fish with him one last time.

It was a summer evening with the windows down and the smell of hayfields whipping my face and Grandpa pressing the pedal of his road-hogging New Yorker to the floor. That big, blue boat just sailed, like nothing, up Route 122–hitting 60 . . . 70 . . . 80 mph to the top of the hill. Then click. He dropped her into neutral and we coasted all the way to the Baker Road, parked, and grabbed our rods.

Through the lush alfalfa we walked single file toward the stream, me a few steps behind out of deference. Grandpa let loose. Toot. Toot. Toot. Toooot. "There!" he said, like he'd made some inarguable point.

We got to his spot under the big willow: a deep, jade pool with tag alders leaning in, shading the cut banks. He settled in and barked, "Friend! Go try that riffle downstream. I've caught a lot of fish in that riffle."

He had never caught a fish in that riffle. No one ever had. Not me nor any of my four brothers before me. The truth is that this was always less about teaching us kids to fish or having someone to fish with than it was about outfishing us and having someone to outfish. But he took us, and we learned. I scrambled a half-mile downstream and worked my way up, catching trout the whole way, reaching Grandpa's spot at dusk.

I sat on the cool bank next to him–he in his lawn chair, his rod on a forked stick. He used a Zebco close-faced combo, 17-pound-test, a couple of split shot, and a nightcrawler threaded onto a "s--t'n Japanese" hook. Whenever he lost a fish, he always blamed his "s--t'n Japanese" hooks, but he was too cheap to buy anything else.

"Well, Friend?" he said.

I showed him the 15-inch brown I'd kept and told him about the other dozen or more smaller ones. For years, my brothers and I had been telling him about all the fish we'd caught and threw back. "Baahh!" he'd always say. They didn't count. They might as well have been pretend fish, or maybe lies. He inspected my 15-incher and grunted. Suddenly his rod was bouncing and waving. He grabbed it and reared back like he was snagged on a tire. I always wondered how many of the poor trout in Grandpa's

pool had been yanked lipless. But this time he was hooked fast. There was a heavy splash in the darkness. Grandpa lunged forward, cranking the Zebco, which complained loudly. There was a moment when it wasn't clear who would win the fight, and then the fish flopped onto the bank and popped free.

"S--t'n Japanese hooks!" Grandpa yelled, as he took a swipe with his boot and miraculously connected, kicking the trout farther up the bank. I dove into the bracken ferns, feeling for the big brown in the dark, and finally held it up in the beam of Grandpa's flashlight. It was a good one. All of 15 inches, probably 16.

Grandpa floored the big Chrysler and up the hill we sailed, bobbing smoothly home. He reached under his seat and came up with a white can printed with block letters: BEER. As we topped the hill, the needle touched 80, and he dropped her into neutral again just as the cop's lights swirled in the rearview.

"Sir, do you know why I pulled you over?"

"Don't you 'sir' me," Grandpa answered, feeling good. "I know your father!"

"Mr. Hurteau, you can't drink and drive."

"Why not? It's my car. It's my beer!"

"Mr. Hurteau—"

"Look at this 17-incher I caught tonight."

The cop let him off, and Grandpa gunned it, though only to 60 this time, and we coasted again down Route 122, right through the stoplight and into the corner gas station.

"How'd you do tonight, Mr. Hurteau?" the attendant asked.

"Caught an 18-incher!"

"You always get the big ones."

"Give me a dollar of unleaded, John," Grandpa said—just enough to get him to the top of the hill twice tomorrow night. He'd be back to lie to John about his next catch.

"Yup, a good night," Grandpa said, then turned and looked at me. "And, ah . . . my grandson here caught a big one, too."

"Yeah, how big?" asked John.

I knew how fast Grandpa's fish could grow. But never my fish. If any-thing, mine shrank.

"Oh . . ." He seemed to think about it. "Probably 15 . . . maybe 15 and a half."

It was the best he could do.

THE BLUEGILL DATE

WILL BRANTLEY

I met Michelle in kindergarten, but I didn't take her bluegill fishing until we were 17. The best bream spot I knew of was Flat Pond, a 2-acre gem hidden in the timber a couple of miles from home. Just getting there was an adventure that required a half-hour trek through woolly, reclaimed mine country, but I didn't mind the walk, or even baiting all the hooks, for the chance to fish with Michelle.

Turns out, Michelle could bait her own hook just fine. We caught a bunch of bluegills, and a bonus 3½-pound largemouth that was the biggest bass Michelle had ever seen. The date was going great—until she discovered her tennis shoes were infested with a hundred or more Lone Star ticks. I dunked her shoes in the pond, which didn't faze the ticks in the slightest. "I'd rather walk home barefoot!" she said.

I followed her, carrying the poles, tackle, and stringer—bass included, since Michelle wouldn't hear of "turning that son of a bitch loose." We walked on, and for a while we didn't say much. When we finally reached the truck, Michelle stopped to rub her bloodied feet. I expected her to list the many reasons why this would be our first and *last* fishing date. Instead, she looked at me and said, "That really is a big old bass."

A girl like that is the kind you don't let go.

Six years later, newly married and flat broke, Michelle and I lived in a one-bedroom apartment near Kentucky Lake. We fished almost every day, usually for bluegills. It wasn't long before a job change carried us to Memphis. The bream fishing in the Tennessee oxbows was even better than the barbecue and blues, but still, it wasn't home. Michelle and I moved back to Kentucky less than two years after we left—but it wasn't to settle down. Michelle wore a bracelet that said Free Spirit, and we lived by that—traveling all over the country, hunting ducks in Louisiana, mountain lions in Colorado, gators and hogs in Florida, and whitetails, turkeys, and flatheads around home. And we still fished for bluegills every spring, same as we'd done since we were 17.

Our folks finally quit asking if we were going to have kids.

One fall afternoon in 2013, I walked into the living room and found Michelle lacing up her hunting boots. A good cold snap had set in, and she told me she wanted to do some rattling in her stand. "Also," she added, "I'm pregnant."

A writer prides himself on always having something to say. Right then, I had nothing.

Our child was due June 18. Toward the end of May, Michelle reminded me that it was the first spring since we were 17 that we hadn't gone bluegill fishing. It didn't matter that she was now weeks beyond the point of doctor-recommended johnboat rides; Michelle wanted to catch some bluegills and she was going fishing, with or without me.

I'd never negotiated waves more carefully than I did that day. Michelle and I struggled with the fishing at first. One bed produced maybe a dozen keepers, but the others were empty—at least, we didn't catch anything from them. Distracted, I reeled in more than a few clean hooks. I kept asking Michelle, "Are you O.K.?"

"If I go into labor, I'll tell you," she eventually said. "Stop asking."

We fished on, and for a while we didn't say much. Michelle braced her swollen ankles on the gunwale of the boat and used her belly as a table to bait her hooks. She kept fishing, and on the first of what would be many "last casts," she found the best bluegill bed of the day. Soon she was catching a fish every minute, and smiling like she was 17 again, back at the Flat Pond. As the sun began to set, our wire basket—now genuinely heavy—buzzed with bream. Usually at the end of the day, Michelle quits first. This time, though, we just kept going till it was too dark to see our corks.

William Anse Brantley arrived a day late, on June 19. People say he has my eyes and Michelle's nose. We've got plenty of stories to tell him, including why there's a 3½-pound bass mounted on the wall. He'll get his chance to learn about bluegill fishing, too.

THE TROUT REUNION

JIM FERGUS

It is the 40th anniversary of the first Boys' Annual Fishing Trip and we have reconvened in Saratoga, Wyoming, to float the North Platte River, a blue-ribbon trout stream. Four friends since college, we are suddenly late-middle-aged men. Truthfully, the trip has not been held every year; over the past decade in particular we have occasionally let it lapse, unable to find a long summer weekend agreeable to all parties. But this year, in honor of the occasion, we have managed to organize the trip, and as we have often done in the past, we have invited two guests, also old pals. Presently, we're following another tradition, which is to dine our first night in town at the venerable Hotel Wolf. Over cocktails, we chat, shoot pool, and look at a time-faded Denver Post review of the hotel on the wall, dated 1982. My byline is on it. That's how long we've been coming here.

In the restaurant we order Wolf Cut prime ribs, gigantic slabs of beef. As only old friends can, we catch up instantly, the years falling away in the spirit of the event. We quickly regress to the immature behavior of our college days, telling vulgar stories in loud voices and laughing riotously.

At a table next to us, an elderly ranch couple dines in silence, presumably having exhausted over the past half century their repertoire of conversational topics. They can't help but overhear us.

One of us now poses a question: "When was the last time you made love to your wife?" Someone answers: "I remember it vividly. It was my birthday, June 13 . . . 1996." Everyone howls . . . except the rancher, who has had enough. He turns his chair and fixes us with an icy stare. The laughter dies; we feel like schoolboys caught in a prank. "Please excuse us, sir," one of us offers. "We got carried away." This seems to satisfy him, as he turns his chair back to resume dinner with his wife. We begin sputtering like kids.

COLORADO SPRINGS, COLORADO
June 1970

We made the pact back in college—J.D., Johann, D.C., and I—four young men preparing to go out into the real world. It went like this: No matter what happened in each of our lives; no matter where we all lived, what obligations and responsibilities we accrued in the coming years, come hell or high water, poverty or riches, we would take a fishing trip together once every summer—for the rest of our lives.

A subclause of the pact was that when one of us hit it big, made his first million, he would treat the others to a trip to New Zealand, Chile, or Argentina—exotic destinations, the promised lands of flyfishing. In the meantime, we had plenty of water to cover on our own continent.

SARATOGA, WYOMING
40th Reunion Trip

We are up before dawn this first morning, in order to be on the river by 7 a.m. We have rented two of Stoney Creek Outfitters' river cottages, steps from the North Platte and next door to the fly shop—all owned and operated by Wyoming native Shilo Mathill, a lean, energetic man in his 30s. Today we will put in at Bennett Peak campground in the foothills, a half hour's drive from Saratoga, and take out 12 miles downstream at Treasure Island in the lower ranch meadowlands.

Our guides—Shilo, Todd, and Rob—unload the three 14-foot drift boats at the ramp, then busy themselves rigging rods, hunched in their seats, intently tying on leaders and flies. They banter among themselves, already in good-natured competition. We sports mill about, somewhat unaccustomed to being pampered in this fashion. Over the years, we can count on less than one hand the number of times we've hired guides.

"Remember when we used to tie on our own flies?" someone remarks.

"Yeah, when we could still see to do it."

KAMLOOPS, BRITISH COLUMBIA
July 1975

From the beginning, there were years in which all four of us were unable to reach consensus on places and dates. Sometimes only two or three made the trip, but that was enough to keep the tradition alive.

J.D. got married early, D.C. went off to be a sailing bum in the Caribbean for a couple of years, Johann and I moved to distant states—all of which created logistical problems. But none of us had exactly traditional starter jobs, and we were still at the age where a nonstop cross-country drive in an old sports car was not only feasible, but fun.

This year, Johann and I were the sole attendees, and we decided to drive from Colorado to Minnesota to fish for bass and pike. From there we wandered into Canada, hung a left onto Highway 1 in Ontario, and drove nonstop through Manitoba, Saskatchewan, Alberta, and on into British Columbia, taking turns at the wheel and laughing with sleep-deprived delirium the entire way. Beyond the fishing, that's what we would remember most about those days, how much we laughed.

In British Columbia, we stayed at a fish camp outside Kamloops. On the first day, we rented a boat and went out on the lake, where we caught a couple of Kamloops rainbows. At the end of the day, we were cleaning our catch when a little girl, maybe 10 years old, approached, dragging a trout longer than her arm. "How'd you do?" she asked, peering up at the table where our two 12-inchers lay.

"Oh, we caught a couple of nice ones," Johann said as we tried to block the girl's view. "You know, for our first day out."

The girl dropped her fish on the wooden walkway; it sounded like a side of beef hitting the floor. "Can I see them?" she asked.

Reluctantly, we held up our trout. "Oh, those are beauties," said the girl, politely. "Now if you're finished cleaning them, could you help me lift mine up onto the table?"

SARATOGA, WYOMING
40th Reunion Trip

It occurs to us as we are seated in our respective boats, one angler in the bow and one in the stern, and as the guides push us off from the boat ramp as if we are conquering emperors, that we have been fishing this river since before any of these young men were even born. As the boats spread out, the sounds of oars dipping, lines stripping from reels, men talking softly, morning birds singing, and the varied tones of the river itself drift out over the water like a symphony. Good lucks are exchanged, plans to meet downriver for lunch made.

Always on the first morning of a fishing trip, there is that wonderful sense of promise, and nothing quite delivers on it like the first fish sighting of the day. In this case, it's a large brown feeding in a back eddy, his dorsal fin and tail breaking the surface as he rolls.

I am paired with J.D. in Shilo's boat. Just because we've been flyfishing for most of our lives, of course, does not make us experts. We grew up in a simpler era, when our fly boxes were stocked with Royal Coachmen, grasshoppers, Adamses, Light Cahills and, my personal favorite, Irresistibles. Sure, we had classic wet flies and streamers and, of course, a few nymphs (including the perennially popular Gold Ribbed Hare's Ears), but for the most part, unlike our guides, we were rather low-tech generalists. Now, when I pull out my gear at the beginning of the season—my ancient vest, an old Hardy reel and Orvis 99 bamboo rod my dad bought me when I was 15—I'm struck by the fact that it's all begun to resemble a museum display of grandpa's stuff.

Neither J.D. nor I have quite limbered up our somewhat out-of-practice casting arms (at least that will be our excuse), and perhaps, too, there is the matter of first-fish jitters. This particular trout appears to be taking emergers, but early on one of us puts it down with a sloppy cast. No matter.

Shilo has plenty of experience with hackers, and with perfect guide's equanimity, he rows us to the next run.

NORTH PARK, COLORADO
July 1978

Around the mid '70s, I purchased a red 1968 Volkswagen camper and pasted a jumping-trout decal on the back. We would park the camper by a creek, pop the top, set up the attachable tent, break out the Coleman stove, and presto: the official movable lodge of the Boys' Annual Fishing Trip.

Somehow all four of us, and sometimes guests, managed to sleep in the camper and tent. One year, while camped on the Michigan River in Colorado's North Park, Johann drew the straw to sleep in the little hammock-like cot that folded out in the pop top. At 6-foot-4, he was not a small man, and the fact that he had drawn the cot caused a good deal of chortling. Late the first night, Johann suddenly started howling in his sleep and began trying to climb down from his perch. The top-heavy camper was rocking like a ship in heavy seas. "Wake up, Johann!" yelled J.D. as he and I tried to extricate ourselves from our mummy bags before we all tipped over, or Johann crushed us in his descent. "You're having a nightmare!"

"Wake up!" I chimed in. "You're sleepwalking!"

"I am awake, you morons!" Johann hollered back. "And I'm not sleepwalking! I've got a leg cramp! Out of my way!"

SARATOGA, WYOMING
40th Reunion Trip

Our boats hopscotch down the river. With the water low and warm, the guides have to work hard for fish, and by this point in midseason, Shilo, Todd, and Rob are all lean as whippets from rowing porky sports who've been bulking up on Wolf Cut prime ribs.

They have two rods rigged for each angler—a lighter weight for dries, a heavier weight for nymphs and streamers. Each rod has a lead fly and a dropper—depending on the line weight, some combination of dries, nymphs, or streamers, with weights and strike indicators where appropriate. To find out where and on what the fish are feeding, one angler fishes one combination of flies, the other something different, thus covering all the bases.

This upper canyon stretch is studded with rocks and boulders, pocket water of fast riffles and runs, and deep pools on the bends. "See that seam between the fast water and the slower? Drop your fly right in there," Shilo instructs J.D. "Perfect. Mend your line. O.K., now give it the twitch of death." Just as J.D. is executing the twitch, which involves wiggling the rod tip to give the nymph action as it rises, a 17-inch rainbow nails his fly.

A mixed bag of browns and rainbows follows, caught on everything from tiny Trico spinners to nymphs to streamers. If the fishing is not exactly hot, it is, for this time of year, consistent. When things slow down, the guides change flies and add or subtract weights with obsessive attention.

In the meantime, a spectacular array of wildlife greets us along the river—redtail hawks and ospreys circle overhead, bald eagles roost in the cottonwoods, deer graze on the banks, woodchucks peer down from the canyon walls, beavers swim across the current, and toward the end of the day, an enormous great horned owl squats on a gravel bar, watching us impassively as we float past.

SARATOGA, WYOMING
August 1982

This was the first year we'd floated the North Platte, and feeling unusually flush, we broke precedent and hired an outfitter. Our guide went by the name "Big Ed." We quickly discovered he was a stolid blowhard who knew little more about fishing this river than we did. Not that the poor fishing was Big Ed's fault; we had come during the dog days when the North Platte had gone low and slack and hot. The fish were holed up in the bottoms of the deepest pools, and we did not yet understand the river well enough to know how to reach them. But Big Ed did not appear to have a clue, other than suggesting that we tie on large metallic Zonkers and fish the foam. It's true that hatching insects get caught in the foam, and that trout frequently feed beneath it, safely hidden from avian predators.

On this trip, however, on the rare occasions when a fish was actually spotted working in the foam, Big Ed would holler "Fish the foam!" Then, careful not to maneuver us within fly-casting range, he would drop the oars, whip out his spinning rig, and plunk a Panther Martin directly on top of the rise, immediately putting the fish down. "Damn, shoulda hooked that one," Big Ed would say, proud of his accuracy with the spinning rod. "Hit the son-of-a-bitch right on the head, didn't I?"

SARATOGA, WYOMING
40th Reunion Trip

After 12 hours on the river this first day, we unlimber our creaky legs at the takeout. One of us complains about tennis elbow from casting, another of a sore shoulder. We are not in tiptop fishing condition. Plus, of course, we're older now, and we watch enviously as the guides, who have done the real work all day, scamper about, securing gear and loading boats onto trailers as if they have energy to burn.

On the drive back to town, plans are made for the next day's fishing. After showers, we sit on the deck of the river cottage, trading tales of fish caught and lost. As always, 15-inchers become 18-inchers, 18-inchers stretch over 20. We tell stories of our own and our boatmates' less than stellar casting performances, of impenetrable leader tangles that would have taken us hours to straighten out, but which the guides repaired like magicians. And we laugh.

SARATOGA, WYOMING
July 1986

Despite the poor fishing that first year on the North Platte, we would come back. By the mid '80s, we began to hold our trip at a regular spot—a huge private ranch that sold, by today's standards, ridiculously inexpensive permits to fish better than 20 miles of the river. North of Saratoga, this stretch of the North Platte was an hour's drive off the highway, through a high-plains desert landscape, over a long, tooth-rattling dirt two-track that crossed the Oregon Trail. We pitched camp in a grove of cottonwood trees by the river, gathered firewood, and if there was enough light, fished the evening hatch, convening back at camp to build a fire, and prep and cook dinner.

A healthy population of rattlesnakes lived on this stretch of the river, and no trip went by without at least one encounter. One morning, while lighting the burner to make coffee, D.C. discovered a large rattler curled up beneath the Coleman stove. Another year, Johann left a tent flap open and a rattler made itself at home on his pillow. And once, while standing in the river fighting a fish, I noticed a snake floating lazily toward me on a collision course. He spotted me just in time to scoot out of my path, arching his head as he passed not 18 inches away, looking me right in the eye, tongue flicking. Far more than tales of fish caught or lost, events such as this would come to define the lore of the Boys' Annual Fishing Trip.

SARATOGA, WYOMING
40th Reunion Trip

On this second day, we are fishing the middle stretch of the river, from Treasure Island, where we took out the day before, to town. Here, the North Platte flows through irrigated hay meadows and ranchlands. Everyone switches boats and fishing partners, so that in the three days each of us will fish with all three guides, each with his own subtly different though no less effective techniques and style. This prompts D.C., who has always been more interested in watching birds than in fishing, to reflect: "You know, I've been flyfishing since I was 15 years old, and now that I'm over 60, I think it's time I learned how to do it right."

NORTHERN COLORADO
September 1996

By the mid '90s we had settled into our 40s. Remarkably, the trip was still more or less intact. But in that inexplicable phenomenon by which free time in general, and summer in particular, seems to get shorter each passing year, some trips got pushed back into fall and morphed into the Annual Cast and Blast. Sometimes the trip went past fishing season and became the Annual

Bird Hunting Trip. The VW camper had long since been retired, and I had upgraded to a 1971 Airstream trailer, which often served as base camp for our outings.

This year was a cast-and-blast. In the cool fall mornings we hunted sage grouse in the high desert flats or jump-shot snipe along a willow-lined creek; in the afternoons, we fished the streams and ranch ponds of my own home country, where we had been casting lines now for two decades, and upon which we had always fallen back when we had neither time nor resources for trips farther afield.

Though only mid September, there was a wintry chill in the air, and in the evenings we lit a fire in the cookstove of my old log cabin. We grilled the day's bag of snipe or grouse over coals, and puttered around the kitchen, squabbling over dinner preparations like old ladies.

SARATOGA, WYOMING
40th Reunion Trip

Eating and drinking well has always been an important element of our trip, and for this reunion we have outdone ourselves. Besides fine beverages, we have brought French cheeses and Italian salamis, smoked trout, choice rib eyes, racks of lamb, farm chickens, and homegrown garden vegetables supplied by one of our guests, Steve, who has attended enough of these trips to have become a full member.

We settle into our roles as only old friends or old married couples can: I prep and issue commands largely ignored, while Johann relaxes on the deck with a glass of Scotch and a cigar. D.C., a notorious shirker, drinks a beer, his head buried in a map of the river. J.D., the Grill Maestro, heats the grill, while our other guest, Robo, lays out an elegant cheese tray. No trip is complete without at least one cooking argument, and this time I engage the Grill Maestro in an argument ongoing for 40 years about the correct doneness of the meat. J.D. likes his medium, I like mine rare.

All is forgiven, however, as dinner is delicious—despite the fact that under my relentless insistence, half the meat is raw. The wine flows and a lively discussion ensues, though tonight we are free of other diners to disturb.

1999–2010

By the late '90s and on into the millennium, our pact began to unravel. Moves, divorces, family illnesses, the deaths of loved ones, professional and personal obligations and financial responsibilities; everybody seemed to be running harder as they entered their fifties. Somewhere along the line, a sea change occurred. Just as it had been assumed that our trip would always take place, now it gradually gained the status of a relic, something to be remembered in old photos. There came a point when we didn't even try to organize it anymore.

But at last, well past the watershed date of July 4, the time when it might be expected that four old friends with a collective mountain of life's detritus between them might be able to agree on dates, a phone call was made. "What do you think about a last-minute 40th anniversary Boys' Annual Fishing Trip?" J.D. asked.

"What's it been," I answered, "four, five years now? I've lost track."

"Something like that."

"O.K., you call D.C., I'll call Johann."

SARATOGA, WYOMING
40th Reunion Trip

This day will be the slowest, but so what? We have all caught fish, and have already deemed this to be one of the best ever reunions, a combination of fish caught, knowledgeable and companionable guides, beautiful landscapes, incredible wildlife, and great food and wine.

Over dinner, we toast the trip, renew our 40-year-old pact, and promise not to let it lapse again. "Hey, when are we going to New Zealand, Argentina, or Chile?" someone asks.

"Yeah, who's going to make that first million bucks so he can take everyone else?"

We chuckle, remembering the dream that seems as far away now as it did then.

There is, finally, the matter of the "Official Theme Song," the first stanza of which was composed years ago around a campfire on this river. It's possible that alcohol was involved. The plan was that each year, we would compose a new stanza, until eventually we had an entire song. Despite attempts over the years, we never got past the first lame verse. Now, J.D. breaks into song:

Pack up the rods, fellas
Sure has been swell, fellas
The rest of us join in: Let's do it agaaaain neeeeext yeeeaaar . . .

And we laugh.

THE LIFE AHEAD

C.J. CHIVERS

The transformation began in a matter of hours.

It started beside a rack of low-priced rods and a display of lures in a sporting-goods store. The selection was skimpy. But to my sons, Jack, 6, and Mick, 4, this was a portal to a secret world. For two years they had been stuck in a city. Now their fishing lives were about to begin. They wanted to know everything. *What is this?* A swimming plug. *And this?* A jig. *What do you catch on jigs?*

We were on an unexpected summer vacation on the Finnish coast, not far below the Arctic Circle in a region bathed in light. I was trying to put together a simple kit for what I hoped would become a season of fishing school. Everything I touched yielded questions: *What are bobbers? Why do we need a net? How does a handline work? What will that huge lure catch?* Pike.

I looked at that plug—a wooden jerkbait, light gray with black spots—and thought of heaving it out over submerged boulder piles populated by striped bass. Jack was looking at it, too. He was old enough to sense it: Only a big fish would smack a lure like that.

"What's a pike?" he said.

We left 30 minutes later with three rod-and-reel combos, a landing net, a small tackle box, and an assortment of sinkers, hooks, bobbers, and lures. Pike would come later. First we would go slow. Down the block was a marine-goods store. We walked in and bought kid-size life preservers and a few yards of rope. Farther down was a shack selling beach toys, where we picked up a wire fish basket and a canister of worms.

On our back porch the boys watched as I spooled reels, assembled the rods, and tied on small, freshly sharpened hooks. My hands moved by habit. I snipped the line with my teeth. My wife, Suzanne, had packed food: sliced apples, ginger cookies, water, and two containers of juice. I shouldered the backpack, picked up the rods, and walked off. The boys followed, firing questions on the way.

"What will we catch, Dad?" Jack asked.

"I don't know," I said. "We'll see."

I knew I should manage expectations before reaching the docks. I had been here two days, and busy most of that time. I knew nothing about fishing this place, except that we were far enough into the archipelago that the water might be less brackish than sweet. "Sometimes you don't catch anything," I said.

"We'll catch something," Jack said.

"Yeah," Mick added. "Look at the water. There's millions."

The harbor, a basin dredged in flats, was a series of wooden docks with slips for pleasure craft. The channel leading to the sea was a few hundred yards away. No one was fishing. Villagers strolled by as we set up. *You three are cute*, their quizzical glances said. *But odd.*

The boys crowded tight as I baited the hooks and flipped them out. "Watch the bobbers," I said. "If they move, you have a fish."

One of the bobbers plunged. Jack pounced on the rod and pulled back. Out of the water flew a yellow perch. It flipped on the dock until I lifted it in my hand—a green-and-yellow gem with orange pectoral fins and bright eyes. Its smell rose around me, grassy and fresh.

"What is it?" Jack asked.

"It's a perch," I said. He saw my smile and grinned back.

I had expected flounder as much as this. Mick grabbed the fish to study. My mind whirred. Yellow perch? These boys are about to learn.

We had traveled to Ekenäs, a town of Swedish-speaking Finns, for the best of reasons. And then we were blessed with luck, though it did not seem so at first.

We lived in Moscow, and Suzanne had been expecting our fourth child. But she could not find a maternity hospital she trusted there. So three weeks before the due date we rode the overnight train to Finland, bound for a hospital with a good reputation. My plan was to set up the family in an apartment, head back to Russia for work, and return for the big day.

Suzanne woke early the first morning with contractions. False labor, we thought. She had delivered three children already. We had seen this pattern before. Within an hour it was clear the labor was not false. We started walking for the hospital with our three children in tow. We had no phone. The town was asleep. We did not know where the hospital was. Soon Suzanne was in advanced labor on the lawn of a gray stone church. I wondered, Would she deliver this baby here? A car came by. I hailed it and we piled inside. The driver, a man in a pressed white shirt and red tie, looked at Suzanne. She was between contractions, perfectly calm. Another contraction seized her. She stiffened and moaned. "This only happens in the movies," he said and put his car into gear. Ten minutes after we arrived at the hospital, William was born.

What did this have to do with fishing? Living in Russia and having William in Finland created certain problems. We could not travel with him to Russia yet, because he had neither a passport nor the visa required to cross a border. And getting a passport and visa would take weeks. All plans were upended. I would not be going back to Moscow this day. We had begun an impromptu vacation, marooned on an island in the northern Baltic Sea.

The idea appeared that evening, as Suzanne and I sat in the apartment's kitchen, gazing at our newborn. A summer-session fishing academy would be held. I would teach the boys to fish, preparing for the lives ahead.

Summer twilights extend nearly to morning in Ekenäs, where drenching rains inland drain past the islands and create eddies in a sweetwater flow.

It was June 18. I sat in the glow planning lessons in fishing and safety skills. Some would be easy, like baiting hooks, setting bobbers, and unhooking and handling fish. Others would take time, like learning to jig.

And a few would be frustrating at first, like developing the timing required to snap out proper casts. There would also be important lessons—including filleting, which required handling a finely sharpened blade—that they would only watch. But fishing is not just an assemblage of skills. It is a mentality, a way of viewing your surroundings in fundamental terms, as a naturalist and a predator alert to the world. I would teach my boys about the food web and the life cycles of whatever fish lived here, and the joys and satisfactions, embedded in their DNA, of harvesting their own food.

At first the perch came slowly. But after a few days of plumbing the harbor, we found patterns—and bigger fish. I sensed that we had stumbled onto a boon. I am a lifelong and essentially addicted fisherman. Proximity to gamefish has influenced where I attended college, where I have worked, and ultimately where my wife and I decided to buy a house in Rhode Island, for our upcoming move back to the United States. And I knew something important as I set out to teach Jack and Mick during this unexpected window in family time: that no matter how many lessons I had in mind, without a cooperative and tasty run of fish, my informal angling academy could flop.

But Ekenäs, as it happened, had yellow perch. And what could be better? Perch are small and handsome and feed in packs. They strike hard but fight lightly. They prey on a range of forage, feed in varied conditions, are comfortable in the shallows, and are not especially selective. They have no sharp teeth, making hook removal safe. They would be my assistants. If I could put the boys near the perch, the perch would do much of the teaching themselves.

Within a week, Jack and Mick were moving from epiphany to epiphany. Mickey, his blond hair trimmed tight and bleaching under the sun, was fishing simultaneously with a rod and with a handline. He handled the second line instinctively, like an ice fisherman of yore, wiggling a small vertical jig with a piece of worm. He quickly fooled a heavy perch, nearly a foot long. It flopped on the dock and he dove on it like a loose football. He was 4 years old, a child adrift in time.

"Jack," he shouted. "Jack! Look!"

At home I opened the basket's door and let a load of perch, perhaps two dozen in all, slide into the sink. Jack and Mick pulled up chairs and climbed up to watch. The sound of a knife being run across a sharpening stone filled the air. My daughter, Elizabeth, came running; she wanted to see, too. She was just past 2 years old and did not yet have the patience or swimming skills to spend long hours on the docks. But she was drawn to the creatures her brothers brought home. "Give me one," she called out. "Boys!"

We are meticulous with fish in our house, and I transferred most of the whole perch into the freezer before I cleaned them, to keep them cool until it was their turn.

I took a larger, thicker fish from the sink—a perch Mick had jigged up—and rested it on the board. Then I slipped the knife in, following the skeletal contours from head to tail. One fillet, grayish-white and with a tracery of fine black lines, was clear. I flipped the fish and removed the meat from the other side.

The pile of fish shrunk and the pile of meat grew. For all the perch's many qualities as an instructional fish, they have another value as well: They are delicious. A basket of cold perch is a natural treat on the order of a basket of peaches still warm from the tree. When we finished with the knife, I took a stack of chilled fillets, dipped them in egg and beer, and rolled them in seasoned flour. The boys pushed the chairs to the stove and watched the muscles that had powered their quarry around the docks sizzle and brown in a skillet of hot olive oil. Then we sat with a mound of small fillets, each one brilliant white and warm inside, feasting with green salad and tall glasses of milk. Their pride was self-evident. The boys were feeding us.

"Mama," Jack said. "We caught these."

"Yes, Jack," Suzanne said. "And you will catch many more."

I marveled at their progress. Once Willie's passport arrived at the embassy in Helsinki, I returned to Russia for work and to pick up our son's visa. When I turned up in Finland again in August, the boys wanted to fish.

They had come a long way in a few weeks. One afternoon on the dock, as Mick and I headed to the comfort station, I looked back and saw Jack, who was watching the rods alone, dash left, bend, pick up a rod, and swing back.

When we returned, he stood quietly, tending our three rods, staring at three bobbers. I pretended not to know. "How's it going?" I asked.

"I caught a fish," he said.

"Really?" I said. "What kind?"

"A perch. It's in the basket."

"Where's your line?"

"I put a worm on and put it back."

His bobber floated 30 feet from the dock.

The lessons had stuck. Jack was already a fisherman. He had caught a fish, unhooked it, lifted the heavy wire fish basket from the water, hand over hand with the rope, and put in his catch—by himself. Then he rebaited and cast the line back. There were things in that sequence I had not yet taught him.

That night, after the last fillets were put up, the fishing tackle stowed, and the boys had showered and gone to bed, I sat in the kitchen, sipping a beer. It was about 11 p.m. Jack padded into the room in his pajamas, carrying a spool of 6-pound-test. He had twisted its tag end into kinks. He had watched me tying clinch knots, Uni knots, and the Palomar. He handed me the spool, determination on his face. He wanted to know how. "Can I have a knot-tying class?" he said.

Late one evening, I slipped Willie into a harness that held him at my chest and grabbed a spinning rod that rested across two nails on the wall. He was 7 weeks old. We had his passport and visa now. Soon we'd head back to Moscow.

We stepped outside. His tiny hands were balled to fists against my shirt. I hummed to keep him still. We stopped on the docks between the Polaris, a tug painted red, and the Suppan II, a dinner vessel that looked as if it might have plied the Mississippi a hundred years ago. The water was deeper here, and fish often suspended near the hulls. My rod dangled a small tin jig, a wafer-thin version of what Norwegians use for cod. I ran my thumb and index finger along the monofilament strand, checking for abrasions, then pulled steadily on the line. "The knot's okay," I said.

Willie watched everything and nothing, mesmerized. I ran the hook across my fingernail—sharp enough to catch.

Out flipped the jig. It hit the water with a plop like a dime tossed into a wishing pool. I watched it juke right, drop, and disappear. Four perch rushed the place where it passed, dorsal fins high. Then they dove. The line went limp. I knew what that meant: One had caught up with it. I snapped the rod back. It bent and stayed down. The fish made a few thumps as I reeled it toward the surface and swung it onto the dock.

"Look," I said. "Perch."

Willie's expression was unchanged. The fish meant nothing to him. I turned the hook out and dropped the fish into the basket.

When we left at 11 p.m., I was carrying a basket of 28 perch and Willie was asleep. I passed through the yard, climbed the creaking steps, dropped the fish into the sink, washed my hands, and placed the baby beside his mother.

The filleting began. It was a task so familiar that my age seemed to fall away. I was no longer a father of four. I was a child again, like my sons and daughter asleep in the other room. My sun-darkened hands worked automatically. My mind seemed empty, lost in the monotony of plenty, as if I were sorting fruit, as if time had stopped when I first started passing blades through fish more than three decades ago. Slice by slice, perch by perch, a ritual in a string of uncountable fish-cleaning sessions that blend together as one.

Two days before we were to leave, Suzanne made an early dinner and packed a bag of snacks. It was mid-August. The first chill of autumn was in the air. By this time Jack and Mick had caught a few hundred perch, and we had packed away meat for winter meals. I hoped now for a graduation exercise. Our landlord, Robert, had given us permission to use his 14-foot boat. The three of us would try to catch a pike.

I had studied the chart, bought a pack of steel leaders, and explained the need for them to the boys. On one rod I snapped on a spoon; on the other a white plug with a red head. I cut the speed about a mile from the harbor and hung the plug over the side, working the throttle until it had just the right wobble. I cast it onto the surface beside the trailing wake and left the bail open. Coils of line left the spool as the boat pulled away. I closed the bail and handed the rod to Jack. "Hold the tip out," I said. "And hold on tight." Jack flexed his body as if he expected to be yanked over the side. Then I cast out the spoon and handed the second rod to Mick. He nodded.

"A pike!" Mick shouted. Sure enough, his rod was bouncing. He handed it to me, excited. The fish stopped fighting immediately. I reeled it close: a big perch.

We trolled on.

Anticipation drained out of the trip during the passing of an hour, and the boys rummaged in the cooler and found the snacks.

"Pay attention," I said. Too long without a strike—they were unconvinced.

We trolled around an island and turned south along the channel, zigging over its edge and then zagging over weed flats to its west. The Suppan II was heading out. It chugged down the channel. Dinner guests stood at its rail and waved. We had become scenery.

Jack's rod lunged hard. "Dad!" he shouted and tried to reel, but the fish was too heavy. He handed the rod to me. The fish came in thrashing, tried to dive under the boat, and then yielded, exhausted, and allowed itself to be led, mouth open, into the net.

"A pike!" Mick shouted. "A pike!"

I lifted it onto the boat. On the Suppan II, where the skipper had idled to watch, they were cheering.

I looked down at this creature in the net, white spots on pine green, its mouth gripping the balsa plug. It was only a 5-pound fish. But I understood what it meant. "We caught a pike!" Mick shouted. "A pike! A pike!"

A few minutes later the boat rose on plane in the golden light. We were headed back to the dock. Our season was over, and with it the first lessons of their fishing lives. The boys' short hair whipped about their foreheads as the boat skimmed along. None of us spoke. We were fishing partners now.

ABOUT THE AUTHORS

WILL BRANTLEY is a regular contributor for *Field & Stream* and fieldandstream.com—known particularly for charming and humorous stories about panfishing, catfish noodling, and bowfishing in the American South. Brantley lives in Kentucky with his wife, Michelle, and their son, William Anse.

MONTE BURKE is a staff writer at *Forbes* magazine, and contributes often to *Field & Stream, Garden & Gun*, and other magazines. He's also author of the bestseller *Sowbelly*, about anglers' obsession with catching the world-record largemouth bass.

BOB BUTZ is an author, magazine writer, and longtime fisherman. Born in Harrisburg, Pa., Butz has written for *Field & Stream, GQ, Outdoor Life*, and other magazines, and has won several awards.

PHILIP CAPUTO began his writing career in 1968 as a general assignment and investigative reporter for the *Chicago Tribune*. He has written 19 books and published dozens of stories for *Field & Stream*, as well as other leading publications, including the *New York Times, National Geographic*, and *Esquire*.

JOE CERMELE was named Fishing Editor of *Field & Stream* in 2011. He contributes regularly to the magazine and is the coauthor of the fishing blog The Lateral Line on fieldandstream.com. He also produces the website's popular and award-winning fishing show, *Hook Shots*.

C. J. CHIVERS is a journalist, author, and former Marine. The winner of a Pulitzer Prize and National Magazine Award, he is a senior writer for the *New York Times*, and writes for *Field & Stream, Esquire*, and other magazines. His book *The Gun*, a history of automatic weapons, was published in 2010 to wide acclaim.

KIRK DEETER is an Editor-at-Large for *Field & Stream* and the coauthor of the flyfishing blog Fly Talk on fieldandstream.com. He has traveled extensively throughout North and South America to fish. His writing has won numerous awards, including "Excellence in Craft" top honors from the Outdoor Writers Association of America for his fishing and conservation stories.

JIM FERGUS is a novelist, essayist, and outdoorsman. He is the author of four novels and two books of nonfiction. His most recent novel, *The Memory of Love*, was published in 2013.

JIM HARRISON is a renowned novelist, poet, and essayist—as well as a lifelong outdoorsman. In addition to *Field & Stream*, he has written for *The New Yorker, Esquire, Sports Illustrated, Playboy*, and more. He lives in both Arizona and Montana.

BILL HEAVEY has worked as a writer for *Field & Stream* since 1993, and is well known for the magazine's back-page column, "A Sportsman's Life." His humorous writing on the outdoors has been collected and published in two volumes: *If You Didn't Bring Jerky, What Did I Just Eat?* and *It's Only Slow Food Until You Try to Eat It.*

DAVE HURTEAU is a Deputy Editor at *Field & Stream* and has worked for the brand, in one capacity or another, for 20 years. Hurteau has hunted and fished throughout much of the country. He is co-author of the *Total Deer Hunter Manual* and is currently working on the upcoming *Total Bow Hunting Manual.*

TED LEESON has been writing about fishing for *Field & Stream* for more than a decade, and has also published several books on the subject. He teaches writing at Oregon State University.

GUY MARTIN has written for *Town and Country, Garden & Gun, Forbes Life, Condé Nast Traveler, The New Yorker,* the *(London) Observer Magazine, Paris Match,* and the *(London) Sunday Telegraph.* His work has been anthologized in *The Best American Sports Writing.*

NATE MATTHEWS is *Field & Stream*'s digital director and online editor, and has contributed dozens of stories, along with hundreds of photographs, for fieldandstream.com. He loves to hunt big striped bass in his home waters around Long Island, N.Y.

KEITH MCCAFFERTY is a novelist and longtime contributor to *Field & Stream.* His survival stories for the magazine have been nominated for numerous National Magazine Awards, and his assignments have taken him as far as the jungles of India and as close to home as his own backyard. He is the author of three mystery novels: *The Royal Wulff Murders, Dead Man's Fancy,* and *The Gray Ghost Murders.*

THOMAS MCGUANE is an award-winning author of more than a dozen novels and short story and essay collections. He is a member of the American Academy of Arts and Letters as well as the Flyfishing Hall of Fame.

JOHN MERWIN wrote for *Field & Stream* for nearly 20 years, from 1994 until his death in 2013, including six years as Fishing Editor. A true legend in the angling world, Merwin wrote and edited 15 books on fishing and was responsible for some of the magazine's most popular fishing stories, including the June 2008 cover story that was nominated for a National Magazine Award.

JONATHAN MILES is a frequent contributor for *Field & Stream* and has been the magazine's Wild Chef columnist since 2004. He is a contributor to *Food & Wine, Garden & Gun,* and many other magazines, and his writing has been selected numerous times in the annual *Best American Sports Writing* anthologies. Also the author of two novels, Miles lives with his family along the Delaware River in rural New Jersey.

T. EDWARD NICKENS is an Editor-at-Large for *Field & Stream*. He is known for his do-it-yourself wilderness adventures and profiles about people and places where fishing and hunting are the heart and soul of a community. He is also the host of the brand's *Total Outdoorsman* and *Heroes of Conservation* online series. Nickens lives in Raleigh, N.C., within striking distance of mountain trout and saltwater flyfishing.

MIKE TOTH is the Executive Editor at *Field & Stream*, and has been with the brand for nearly 20 years. A serious and longtime angler, Toth enjoys chasing striped bass, bluefish, and fluke from his kayak around his home waters of New Jersey. He is the author of *The Complete Idiot's Guide to Fishing Basics*.

ABOUT THE EDITOR

COLIN KEARNS is a Deputy Editor at *Field & Stream*. A devoted fisherman, Kearns grew up in Missouri, chasing trout and smallmouth bass, but it wasn't until he moved to Montana—working for a fly shop on the Missouri River—when, for him, fishing went from passion to obsession. Before *Field & Stream*, Kearns was an editor at *Salt Water Sportsman* for three years. He lives in New York with his wife, Amanda—who kindly overlooks all of the fishing tackle he has crammed in their small apartment.

ABOUT THE MAGAZINE

As the world's leading outdoor magazine, *Field & Stream* has celebrated the complete outdoor experience, including hunting, fishing, conservation, and wilderness survival, for more than 100 years. With great stories, compelling photography, and sound advice, the magazine has been awarded numerous national magazine and writing awards while honoring the traditions hunters and outdoorsmen have passed down for generations.

weldon**owen**

VP, Publisher Roger Shaw
Finance Director Philip Paulick
Associate Publisher Mariah Bear
Editor Bridget Fitzgerald
Creative Director Kelly Booth
Art Director William Mack
Production Director Chris Hemesath
Associate Production Director Michelle Duggan

Typesetting by Fortuitous Publishing

FIELD & STREAM

Executive Vice President Eric Zinczenko
Editor-in-Chief Anthony Licata
Executive Editor Mike Toth
Managing Editor Jean McKenna
Deputy Editors Dave Hurteau, Colin Kearns, Slaton L. White
Copy Chief Donna L. Ng
Senior Editor Joe Cermele
Assistant Editor Kristyn Brady
Design Director Sean Johnston
Photography Director John Toolan
Deputy Art Director Pete Sucheski
Associate Art Directors Kim Gray, James A. Walsh
Production Manager Judith Weber
Digital Director Nate Matthews
Online Content Editor David Maccar
Online Producer Kurt Shulitz
Assistant Online Editor Martin Leung

2 Park Avenue
New York, NY 10016
fieldandstream.com

Field & Stream and Weldon Owen are divisions of

BONNIER

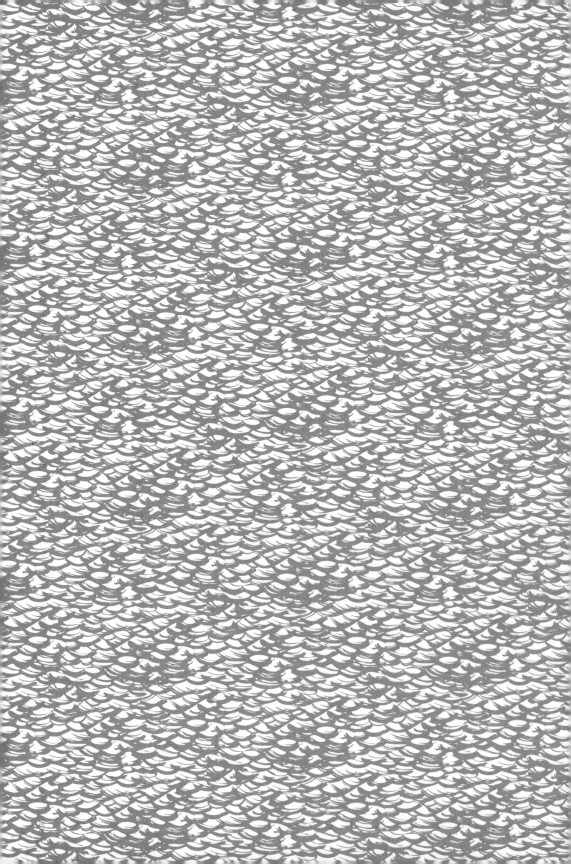